The BOOJUM and ITS HOME

Idria columnaris Kellogg and its Ecological Niche

The BOOJUM

and ITS HOME

ROBERT R. HUMPHREY

THE UNIVERSITY OF ARIZONA PRESS
Tucson Arizona

About the Author . . .

ROBERT R. HUMPHREY's intensive field observation and study of the Boojum from 1967 to 1971 underlines his conviction that in-depth studies of plants as well as animals are sorely needed for man's better understanding of his universe. A studious researcher of Arizona vegetation since the 1930s with the U.S. Forest Service and the U.S. Soil Conservation Service, he developed an expertise that carried him subsequently into Mexico, Brazil, Nigeria, and Saudi Arabia. In the span of years after joining the University of Arizona faculty in 1948 through becoming professor emeritus of Watershed Management and professor of Biological Sciences, he has written and subsequently revised his works, *Arizona Range Grasses* and *The Desert Grassland* (UA Press, 1968, 1970) and has authored many other publications on ecology, grasses, forage plants, and range management.

THE UNIVERSITY OF ARIZONA PRESS

I. S. B. N. 0-8165-0436-9
L. C. No. 73-87548

*This work is appreciatively dedicated to
Dr. William S. Cooper who first introduced
me to the boojum and to ecology, and to
Dr. Forrest Shreve under whose deft guidance
at the Carnegie Desert Laboratory my love of
the desert was born and flourished.*

Contents

ILLUSTRATIONS

MAPS

TABLES

Foreword

THE DEGREE OF ENJOYMENT one obtains from plants and animals and from the ecosystem of which they are a part is heightened by familiarity. The only animals that we usually know intimately are those we may have as pets, and the only plants we may feel an empathy for are often only those we may be trying to grow in pots and gardens. How little we sometimes know about these plants' needs is indicated by the struggle they often have barely even to survive under our care. And, finally, how much less, even, do we usually know of the native plants about us.

Among botanists, themselves, the taxonomist is often aware largely of genetic relationships, and then principally of specific groups; the morphologist, of certain morphological characteristics; the anatomist of internal structure; and the ecologist of energy relationships. Each of these "ologies" may contribute toward understanding a particular kind of plant as an individual or as a member of an ecosystem. None of them, however, can give one the intimate, almost personal feeling for and understanding of a species that is so often lacking. Only by long-continued study of a species in its native habitat can such an understanding be attained.

The boojum tree or cirio *(Idria columnaris* Kell.) was one for which I developed a personal, long-standing interest dating back to the early 1930s. I first saw it growing in its native habitat in 1930. At the time I was interested in ecological anatomy, and during the next three years I spent much time in a study of the anatomy of *Idria* and the closely related ocotillo *(Fouquieria splendens* Engelm.).

This initial acquaintanceship gave birth to a desire to know more about the plant in its home environment, a desire that could not be realized for many years.

It has long been my conviction that we need thorough, in-depth studies on many species of plants similar to those that have been made on some animals. Whether the plants involved may or may not have particular economic significance is beside the point; any organism may become of interest to a wide audience when much is known about it. And the more that is known, the greater and wider this interest may become. I hoped, therefore, that an in-depth study of this striking member of the plant kingdom and of the desert in which it grows might contribute to a real understanding and enjoyment of the species and the ecosystems of which it is a unique constituent.

It was a part of this hope that some light might be thrown on the question of why, even though the boojum thrives when transplanted even to distant, climatically different locations, its natural range is restricted to a small portion of Baja California and Sonora in Mexico. Perhaps the answer will never be fully known, but an analysis of the rather short-period and all-too-sparse climatic records, of seed production, and of habitat and seedling establishment data appear to have given us at least a partial clue.

The field investigations were carried out during many trips to Baja California and Sonora. These were made at all seasons of the year, largely during the period 1967 to 1971, to observe *Idria* and the associated vegetation under the widest possible variety of climatic and growing conditions. These conditions varied from summer heat and drought to winter cold and torrential rains and, in one instance, snow.

Precipitation in the land of the boojum is low and uncertain, although occasionally so heavy as to make the roads impassable for short periods. Some roads, regardless of weather, are recommended only for four-wheel-drive vehicles. After a heavy rain they are impassable even for these cars.

Water, potable or not, is available at only a few places, and there were many times when we were thankful for our 26-gallon supply. When we were near the Pacific or the Gulf of California we invariably used sea water for bathing, dishwashing, and some cooking, reserving our supply of fresh water for making coffee or for drinking "straight." Two people working in the heat of a desert summer sun require a surprising amount of water in order to function effectively.

One always hopes he will not be faced with a serious emergency, such as a car breakdown; still, the roads being what they are (see p. xv), and cars and drivers being fallible, a serious breakdown is always possible. There are no garages or car parts available, and the closest source of replacements for our work in "Baja" were at Tijuana or Mexicali, some 200 to 400 miles to the north.

For transportation we used — and sometimes of necessity abused — a Volkswagen Campmobile, even though the lack of a four-wheel-drive vehicle occasionally restricted our movements. But on the whole,

"Improved" coastal highway (Mexico Route 1) between El Socorro and El Rosario, as it appeared in October 1971.

despite the heavy dust, soft sand, deep mud, and steep rocky hills, the VW served our purposes well, and we never had any problem that delayed us for more than a week at any one time.

Perhaps the closest we came to a bad situation was once when the car — with a burned-out starter — became mired axle-deep for 24 hours in apparently bottomless mud, 55 miles from the closest habitation. This was a remote area on the Pacific coast where we saw no cars for four days, and where it looked as though no one had passed for many weeks.

Another time we were marooned on a temporary island in the center of a normally dry lake bed. Heavy rains during the night made travel impossible, and there was nothing to do except wait for the rains to stop and the waters finally to recede. This episode was a nuisance, but it posed no real hazard as we were well stocked with food and water. Fortunately, the rains quit after a time, and we sat there for only three days in place of what could have been three or more weeks.

A third experience involved failure of the car's ignition system on a rarely visited portion of the Pacific coast. By the third day the water supply ran low, and the best choice seemed to be to leave my wife as camptender while I walked back toward the closest town, 55 miles to the south. A day and a half and 40 miles later, help appeared in the form of a cattle truck and three vaqueros. A long drink of warm brackish water and a ride the last 15 miles were equally welcome.

This investigation was formally initiated August 1, 1967 under National Science Foundation Grant B7-1685R. A few data collected prior to that time have been included, but the study would not have been possible without the financial support of the National Science Foundation.

Supplemental financial assistance was obtained from the Belvedere Scientific Fund of San Francisco, and, through Dr. J. Rodney Hastings, at the University of Arizona, from an Office of Naval Research Grant. The Belvedere Fund contribution made it possible to obtain essential climatological data and to lay the groundwork in Mexico City for obtaining aerial photographs. The ONR funds were used for purchase of the aerial photographs and publication of the climatological data. These supplemental funds have contributed in no small way to the success of the project, and I voice a very real sense of appreciation for those who helped by making them available.

Much of the inspiration has been provided by my wife, Roberta. Her long-suffering endurance of the ups and downs of many months and miles in the field, her never-ceasing diligence and energy, her cheerful cooperation and forbearance have gone a long way toward making the study not only possible, but more than ordinarily enjoyable. On the secretarial end, her many days at the typewriter, typing and retyping the manuscript, and in indexing and proofreading, also have been invaluable.

I owe a debt of gratitude to Miss Martha L. Noller and Dr. Floyd G. Werner of the University of Arizona, Department of Entomology, for preparation and classification of the insects involved in the pollination analysis.

Several individuals have been extremely helpful from time to time in the identification of plants. For this I am particularly grateful to Drs. Raymond M. Turner and Charles T. Mason, Jr. for their assistance with flowering plants and to Drs. Elizabeth A. Duewer, John W. Thomson, and Elmer R. Canfield for their help with the lichens.

I am also indebted to my son, Dr. Alan B. Humphrey of the University of Arizona College of Medicine, for his assistance and advice on matters statistical.

Finally, I would like to thank Marshall Townsend, Elizabeth Shaw, Douglas Peck, and others of the University Press who have facilitated publication of the study, particularly Gale Monson for his fine and painstaking final editing of the manuscript.

R. R. H.

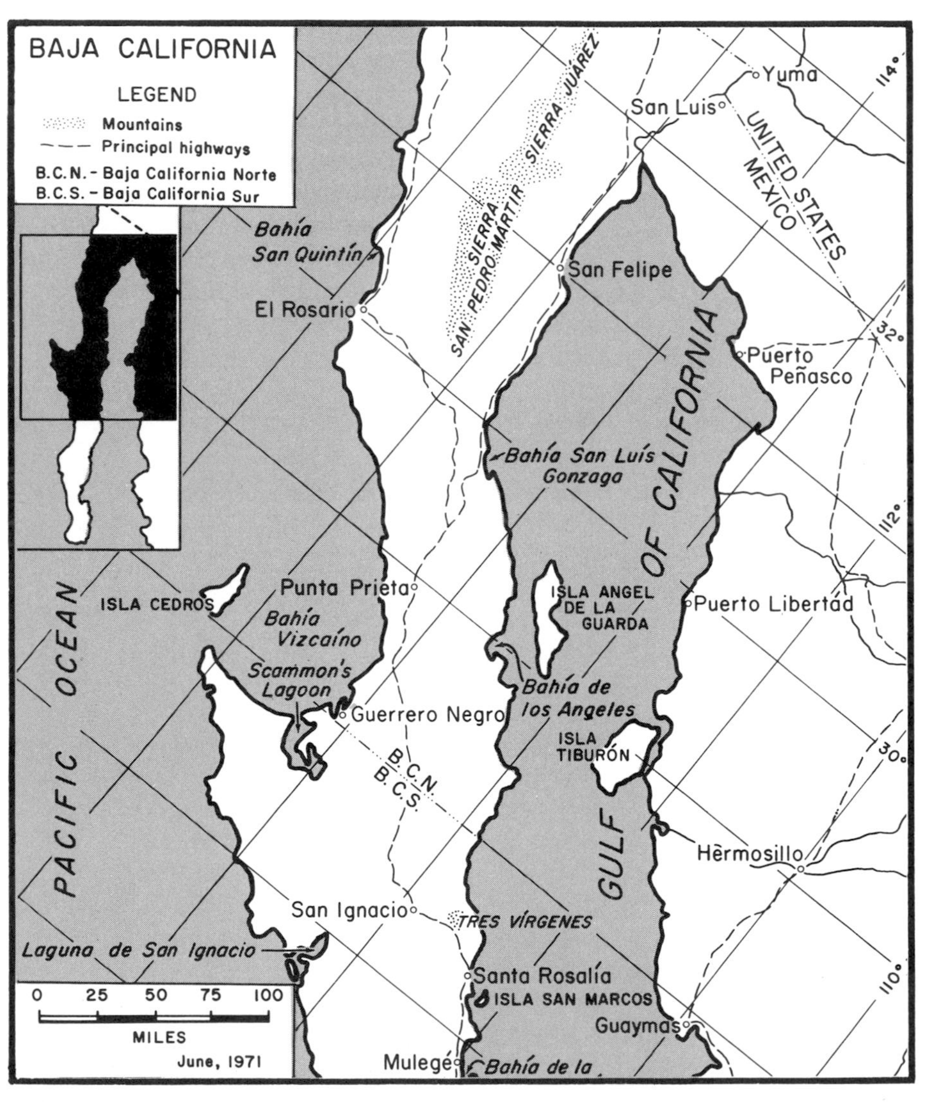
BAJA CALIFORNIA
LEGEND
Mountains
Principal highways
B.C.N. - Baja California Norte
B.C.S. - Baja California Sur
Yuma
114°
San Luis
SIERRA JUÁREZ
SIERRA SAN PEDRO MÁRTIR
UNITED STATES
MEXICO
Bahía San Quintín
San Felipe
El Rosario
32°
Puerto Peñasco
GULF OF CALIFORNIA
Bahía San Luís Gonzaga
112°
PACIFIC OCEAN
ISLA CEDROS
Punta Prieta
ISLA ANGEL DE LA GUARDA
Puerto Libertad
Bahía Vizcaíno
Scammon's Lagoon
Bahía de los Angeles
Guerrero Negro
ISLA TIBURÓN
30°
B.C.N.
B.C.S.
Hermosillo
San Ignacio
TRES VÍRGENES
Laguna de San Ignacio
Santa Rosalía
110°
ISLA SAN MARCOS
0 25 50 75 100
MILES
Guaymas
June, 1971
Mulegé
Bahía de la

1

Salient Physical Characteristics of Baja California

The Baja California Peninsula has been graphically and often imaginatively described by both professional and nonprofessional writers so many times that no attempt will be made here to do more than touch briefly on a few of its chief characteristics.

There is a surprisingly large body of written material pertaining to this arid and isolated peninsula. Ellen C. Barrett (1957), during the seven-year period from 1949 to 1956, compiled a bibliography of 2,873 items pertaining to Baja California and the adjacent islands. Her earliest references date back to 1535; the most recent bring us up to 1956. Her coverage is broad, as suggested by the title page: "A Bibliography of Historical, Geographical and Scientific Literature Relating to the Peninsula of Baja California and to the Adjacent Islands in the Gulf of California and the Pacific Ocean." Much has been written since her book was published, but the book still is probably nearly complete for the 421-year period included.

Location and size

The Peninsula of Baja California is oriented in a southeasterly direction from its boundary with "Alta" California and is roughly 800 miles in length. In width it varies from between 25 and 150 miles, and in elevation it ranges from sea level to about 10,000 feet. It is separated from the mainland of Mexico by the Gulf of California, which in turn varies in width from about 50 to 150 miles (Map I).

The Gulf of California: terminology

The Gulf of California is shown on early maps as the Sea of Cortez or the Vermillion Sea. Even today it is often appropriately called the Sea of Cortez or *El Mar de Cortez* in honor of the Spanish conqueror of Mexico, Hernando Cortez. Cortez, from his base at Zacatula on the west coast of Mexico, at intervals sent out ships to explore the northern coast, landing in person with three ships at La Paz in 1535 in an ill-fated expedition. Four years later he equipped an expedition under Francisco de Ulloa to continue exploration of the Gulf. It was Ulloa, in appreciation of his benefactor, who called the Gulf *El Mar de Cortez* (Clavijero, 1937; Cannon et al., 1966).

Reference to the gulf as the Vermillion Sea derives from the rich vermillion aspect it often assumes from the reflected color of the sky at sunrise or sunset. This designation dates back at least to 1719 and may have been used earlier. An interesting French map reproduced in "The Sea of Cortez" (Cannon et al., 1966) shows the peninsula as the island that it was commonly believed to be at that time, with the gulf labeled *Mer de Californie ou Mer Vermeille*.

Of the various names by which this body of water has been known, I confess a preference for the Sea of Cortez or even the Vermillion Sea. However, to avoid confusion I have not used these terms, but have adhered, instead, to the better known but less picturesque Gulf of California.

Geology

The whole of Baja California consists of the Peninsular Ranges Province, one of four geological provinces that include or border the Gulf of California (Allison, 1964). The Mexican mainland bordering the gulf to the east is classified as the Sonoran Desert Province from the Yaqui River (lat. 27° 39′ N) north, and as the Pacific Coastal Province from there south (Allison, 1964; Rusnak & Fisher, 1964). The disjunct *Idria* population on the mainland near Puerto Libertad is included in the Sonoran Desert Province.

Most of the northern half of the peninsula, essentially the Sierra Juarez and Sierra San Pedro Mártir, as well as the Sierra Victoria area of the Cape region near the southern end, is composed of Mesozoic granites or older metamorphic rocks. According to Allison (ibid., p. 12):

> Late Mesozoic granitic rocks, collectively called the Peninsular Range batholith . . . , and variously metamorphosed older rocks form principal elevations of the northern part of the Peninsular Ranges province. Similar granitic rocks at the southern end of the Baja California peninsula in the Sierra Victoria, and at Cape San Lucas, are considered to be closely related. . . .

Between these two granitic mountain masses occurs a variety of younger rocks of various origins and ages ranging from sandstones, siltstones, limestones, and various clastics, including breccias and conglomerates, to volcanics, some of very recent origin.

Fig. 1.1. Tres Vírgenes volcanic peaks as seen from the west.

The Cerro Tres Vírgenes area between San Ignacio and the gulf provides the most striking of the volcanic flows. The peaks of the now quiescent Volcán Las Tres Vírgenes dominate the landscape, rising to a height of 6,550 feet, more than 5,000 feet above the general basal plain (fig. 1.1). Extensive lava flows partially surround the peaks, many of them appearing to have cooled only yesterday. Old fumaroles are abundant in the old flows adjacent to the mountain, indicating an extensive area of former volcanic activity. According to Shreve (1951), inhabitants of the area report that the volcano was active in 1790. Nelson (1922, p. 60) says the last eruption was reported to have occurred in 1846. Whether or not either of these reports is correct, many of the flows, although on rather level ground, have developed little soil even today and support either very sparse vegetation or none at all (figs. 1.2, 1.3).

Durham and Allison (1960) have proposed that "the peninsula of Baja California and the Gulf of California were probably recognizable after the mid-Cretaceous orogeny, perhaps 100 million years ago." Since then the area of the peninsula has expanded or contracted, and the shoreline has been modified with changes in land level or as a result of sedimentation from the Colorado River. Not until the beginning of the Pleistocene epoch, however, some two to four million years ago, did it assume essentially its present outline.

The evolutionary development of the Gulf of California and the Peninsula of Baja California has been a topic of intensive investigation

Fig. 1.2. Lava flows southwest of the Tres Vírgenes peaks, with elephant trees growing in a slight depression not covered by lava.

Fig. 1.3. Tres Vírgenes peaks as seen from almost due south. Characteristic lava flow almost devoid of vegetation in the foreground.

in recent years. Research and subsequent publications by Larson, Menard, and Smith (1968); by Moore and Buffington (1968); and by Anderson (1971), indicate a rather recent origin resulting from continental drift. In this process, Baja California has "rafted" away from the mainland during the last four to six million years as a result of ocean floor spreading. A proto-Gulf of California presumably existed about four to ten million years ago during the Late Miocene and Pliocene times. Prior to this, the peninsula lay adjacent to the mainland south of Puerto Vallarta, some 170 miles south of its present tip. On the basis of these studies, it has moved north and west some 170 and 125 miles respectively.

Lack of specialized training often requires that many things be accepted on confidence in the research and conclusions of others. One of these in my own case is the migration of continents, or even parts of continents, over great distances. And so it is in the case of the foregoing account of the development of the Gulf of California, and the formation and movement away from its place of birth of the Peninsula of Baja California. This does, however, appear to have occurred, and, as an accepted fact, it provides a basis for some extremely thought-provoking analyses of present-day plant-and animal mainland and peninsular distributions. Ideas for additional investigations should occur as "spin-offs" from current research.

General climatic characteristics of Baja California

Sources of climatic data

Until recently there were few reliable climatic data for Baja California. This resulted in part from the isolation of the peninsula, but in large part because the arid climate made settlement of most of the area difficult or impossible. Because of the consequent low agricultural potential and the paucity of streams, springs, or wells that would facilitate settlement, there was apparently little economic justification for obtaining detailed climatic data.

The Jesuit padres, other early explorers, various travelers, and scientists contributed occasionally to a knowledge of the climate of various parts of the peninsula. At best, though, these reports were spasmodic and applied to restricted areas. The first general discussion of the climate of the whole of Baja California was that of Nelson (1922). His personal observations on the climate were made during 1905 and 1906 when he and Edward A. Goldman were conducting an exploration of the peninsula for the U. S. Bureau of Biological Survey. These observations were presumably supplemented by information from the earlier occasional accounts.

Despite the almost total lack of measurements on which to base his descriptive report, subsequent quantitative data have proved Nelson's account to be surprisingly accurate. It provides an extremely usable and comprehensive, even though brief, description of the climate of the various geographical regions of Baja California.

Shreve (1951), with little more to draw on in the way of quantitative data than Nelson, also described the climate of the peninsula with a high degree of accuracy. A few precipitation and temperature data (Contreras, 1941; Vivo and Gomez, 1946) that had not been recorded at the time of Nelson's report were available to Shreve, but neither his text nor bibliography indicate that he was aware of these, or that they were used. His description of the climate was probably based largely on Nelson's earlier work, supplemented by his own observations and those of his associates. In part, also, his account must have been deduced from his extensive knowledge of the vegetation and climate-plant relationships.

More recently the Mexican government, primarily through two climatological agencies, the *Servicio Meteorologico Mexicano* and the *Secretaria de Recursos Hidraulicos,* has installed a rather dense network of stations well-distributed throughout northwestern Mexico, including Baja California. Precipitation and temperature data from these have been assembled and summarized as the University of Arizona Institute of Atmospheric Physics Technical Reports Nos. 14 and 15 (Hastings, 1964) and Nos. 18 and 19 (Hastings and Humphrey, 1969). The accuracy of these records has been indicated by Hastings (1964) as follows:

> Several considerations suggest that, like any climatological observations presented for the first time, these should be treated cautiously until use has established their merit. In the first place, many of the observations were made from nonrecording instruments, a method that places a premium on the accuracy and reliability of individual observers. Furthermore, it was not possible in the limited time available in Mexico City, without the aid of punch cards and a computer, to check the monthly summaries against daily reports. Finally station histories are sketchy; almost certainly some of the records contain inhomogeneities.

Other recent publications of particular interest to the ecologist include Garcia's (1964) proposal for modification of Köppen's Climatic Classification as adapted to conditions in Mexico; the more recent, more detailed study of climatic conditions in Baja California prepared jointly by Enriqueta Garcia and Pedro A. Mosino (Garcia and Mosino, 1968); and the analysis of seasonal precipitation regimes by Hastings and Turner (1965). The serious student of Baja California and its climate cannot afford to overlook any of these three analytical studies.

As it has not been the primary purpose of this present work to cover the whole of Baja California, but rather to treat in detail only that portion lying roughly between the 27th and 30th parallels of latitude, no attempt is made to discuss, except cursorily, the climate of the whole peninsula. For a more detailed and more technical discussion, the publications mentioned in the preceding paragraph are recommended.

Climatic classifications

The outstanding climatic characteristic of Lower California is its aridity. Of essentially equal importance, however, is its variability, not only from one region to another, but from season to season and from year to year. It can truly be said of most of the peninsula that the most consistent feature of the climate is its inconsistency. This would appear to result from a number of interacting variables, including a wide latitudinal range; extreme differences in elevation; location between the relatively shallow, warm waters of the Gulf of California and the cool, deeper waters of the Pacific Ocean; and the fact that the northern and western portions receive most of their precipitation in the winter while the southern and eastern portions have summer maxima.

Although used as an explanation of two widely disjunct regions of minimum rainfall in Baja California, a statement by Hastings and Turner (1965) also provides a condensed analysis of the meteorological complexities that underlie this variability.

> Lower California lies at the southern edge of the system of winter cyclones that are imbedded in the westerlies and that play so important a part in weather farther north; it lies at the western edge of the monsoons originating in the Gulf of Mexico and dominating northern Mexico in summer; it lies at the northeastern edge of the complex of tropical storms and hurricanes that range across the eastern North Pacific in autumn; it lies at the western limit of fall activity in the easterlies. The peninsula falls consistently under the dominance of none of these regimes and fitfully under the influence of all four. During one year the winter cyclones may reach unusually far south; during another, the summer monsoons may extend west of their usual range. And at frequent intervals the peninsula, particularly in the south, may be buffeted by tropical cyclones. Baja California's participation in all of the regimes, its clear dominance by none, the variable interplay of the four systems from one year to the next — these are factors responsible for the lack of more systematic gradients in the isohyets of mean annual precipitation and for the disjunct centers of dryness.

Hastings and Turner (ibid.), patterning after Shreve's earlier work, divided the peninsula into six phytogeographic provinces; Garcia and Mosino (ibid.), solely on a basis of climate, into three. As would be expected, the phytogeographic classification shows the closer correlation between climate and vegetation; the climatic, on the other hand, may be more consistent with regard to some of the climatic features. Neither treatment, however, detracts from the validity of the other.

The phytogeographic classification divides the peninsula into four desert provinces (the Lower Colorado Valley and the Central Gulf Coast on the eastern slope and the Vizcaíno and Magdalena on the Pacific) and two non-desert (the San Pedro Mártir in the north and the Giganta-Laguna in the south). The climatic characteristics of each are then analyzed on a basis of four arbitrarily designated three-month seasons in which "winter means December, January and February; spring: March, April and May; summer: June, July and August; fall: September, October and November."

Garcia and Mosino's climatic analysis divides the peninsula into the Northwest, Central, and Southeast provinces. Each is characterized by certain parameters of precipitation and temperature. Thus, the Northwest Province has a winter rainfall regime with more than 36 percent of the year's total falling during January, February, and March. The annual mean monthly temperature range is narrow, ranging from 45 F to 57 F. The Central Province has two rainy periods, summer and winter, and has a temperature range of 57 F or more. In the Southeast Province, the bulk of the precipitation occurs during the summer (July, August, and September). Here, as in the Northwest, there is a rather small mean annual temperature range, from 45 F to 57 F.

Climatic regions

Regardless of soil, exposure, slope, and other factors, most plant growth in deserts is controlled largely by climate. And of the major components of climate, including precipitation, temperature, wind direction and velocity, and relative humidity, precipitation is usually the most critical. All are obviously interrelated in varying degrees, but insofar as maximum importance may be ascribed to any one, that one is precipitation.

The broader climatic aspects for purposes of this study are based on a separation of the peninsula into major characteristic precipitation areas. These are:

A. The Pacific Coast
   1. The northern coast
   2. The central and southern coast
B. The Gulf Coast
   1. The northern coast
   2. The central and southern coast
C. The Interior

As these areas are also characterized by climatic elements other than precipitation, they constitute rather broad bases for zones of plant distribution and phenological responses.

The Pacific Coast

Precipitation. The entire Pacific coastal area of Baja California is relatively cool due to the prevailing northwest winds that sweep inland from the cool waters of the Pacific. The northern half of the coast, in particular, is often covered in the summer by a low cloud cover during much of the morning. These clouds may sweep inland some miles, often reaching the ground as fog. This condensation, which is due to a summer temperature inversion, may also occur, but usually does so less frequently, during the winter.

The combination of reduced insolation during the warmest period of the year with a high relative humidity and low temperatures, even though accompanied by rather constant winds, has a marked ameliorating effect on the climate, and consequently on both plant and animal life. The flowering plants consist largely of low-growing species, or, where such normally tall species as *Idria columnaris* or *Pachycormus discolor* approach the coast, they are usually so dwarfed as to bear little resemblance to their inland forms.

The Pacific coast of the peninsula receives little precipitation as is indicated by the mean annual rainfall for 13 coastal stations of only 4.74 inches (table 1.1). The extreme northwest coast and the extreme southwest get considerably more than the rest of the area. Excluding Ensenada (11.02 inches) and Cabo San Lucas (9.30 inches) reduces the mean to 3.76 inches, a figure that more truly represents the general coastal situation.

At least as far south as lat. 26° N, the greater part of the precipitation falls during the five months from November through March, and the bulk of this during December, January, and February. The period from May through September is usually completely without precipitation, the Pacific Coast and immediately adjacent areas almost never receiving any effective moisture. El Socorro (lat. 30° 20′ N), for example, selected as typical of this portion of the coast, has never received any measurable precipitation in May, June, or July during the ten-year period of record, and only once in August and once in September has there been measurable rainfall.

South of Bahía Magdalena, at roughly lat. 24° 30′ N, the greater part of the precipitation falls in the summer, the heaviest rains occurring during the periodic hurricane-type disturbances or *chubascos* that originate off the coast of Mexico below lat. 15° N. The summer monsoon, which is so dominant a feature of the summer months in Sonora, Sinaloa,

TABLE 1.1

Precipitation and temperature data for 13 Pacific coast, Baja California, weather stations *

Station	*Years of Record*	*Latitude* (deg. min. sec. N)	*Precipitation* (inches)	*Temperature* (mean-annual degrees F)
Ensenada	56	31-53-00	11.02	62.1
Colonia Guerrero	17	30-44-00	5.78	59.9
El Socorro	10	30-20-00	5.42	62.4
El Rosario	12	30-03-30	3.74	62.1
Vizcaíno	8	27-59-00	3.14	65.8
Bahía Tortugas	11	27-42-30	3.77	68.5
Punta Abreojos	10	26-44-00	3.00	70.1
San Juanico	8	26-16-00	2.52	70.0
La Poza Grande	24	25-50-30	2.47	68.0
Bahía Magdalena	30	24-38-00	2.90	70.5
La Aguja	5	23-59-00	1.96	72.3
Todos Santos	30	23-26-30	6.66	71.6
Cabo San Lucas	25	22-53-00	9.30	75.7
Average			4.74	67.6

*Data from Hastings and Humphrey, 1969.

and Arizona, affects southern Baja California only slightly, and were it not for the *chubascos* there would be as little summer rainfall in this area as there is elsewhere along the Pacific coast of the peninsula.

Temperature. The generally cool temperatures along the west coast of Baja California are indicated by the mean annual of 67.6 F for 13 coastal stations (table 1.1). These stations have been maintained for varying lengths of time, ranging from a minimum of six years to a maximum of 59 and an average of 21.

July, August, and September are usually the warmest months along the Pacific coast. The July mean-maximum readings, for example, fall between 66 and 82 F, with a mean of 74; those for August between 68 and 85 F, with a mean of 76; and those for September between 67 and 88 F, with a 76 average.

January and February are the coolest months and have identical monthly means of 61 F. December and March are slightly warmer, each with means of 63 F.

There is a distinct and progressive warming trend during each of these four months with distance southward. The December mean monthly temperature at Cabo San Lucas, for example, is 14 degrees higher than

TABLE 1.2

Precipitation and temperature data for 9 Gulf of California, Baja California, weather stations *

Station	*Years of Record*	*Latitude* (deg. min. sec. N)	*Precipitation* (inches)	*Temperature* (mean annual degrees F)
San Felipe	24	31-02-00	2.23	75.2
San Luis Gonzaga	1	29-49-00	1.92	74.3
Bahía de Los Angeles	13	28-53-30	2.90	73.8
El Barríl	11	28-17-30	4.66	73.6
Santa Rosalía	51	27-19-00	4.11	74.7
San Lucas	22	27-09-30	5.93	71.1
Mulegé	43	26-53-30	4.33	73.0
Loreto	26	26-00-30	5.56	76.1
La Paz	50	24-10-00	7.05	75.0
Average			4.30	74.1

*Data from Hastings and Humphrey, 1969.

that at Ensenada, while January is 13 degrees higher, February 11 degrees, and March 12 degrees.

The Gulf Coast

Precipitation. An average of 13 weather stations on the Pacific coast and nine on the gulf indicates that both of these coastal areas receive about the same amount of rain, 4.74 and 4.30 inches respectively (tables 1.1 and 1.2). As we have seen for the Pacific, however, so it is also along the gulf; the amount received varies greatly from place to place.

The driest area of the entire peninsula lies in the northeast corner, in the Colorado River drainage. An average of five stations in this area (Kilómetro 50, El Mayor, Colonia Juárez, Delta, and Bataques) have a mean annual precipitation of only 1.67 inches (Hastings and Humphrey, 1969a). Although none of the stations here is on the gulf, all are within a few miles of the Colorado River; none is more than 65 feet above sea level, and with little doubt they receive about the same rainfall as the extreme northern end of the gulf coast. The total gradually increases toward the south (table 1.2), although it will be noted that even at La Paz, some 600 miles south of the head of the gulf, there is a mean annual of only 7.05 inches.

Although both coasts receive similar precipitation totals, the climate of the two areas is distinctly dissimilar, due largely to differences in temperature and prevailing relative humidity levels. The Pacific coast, despite the aridity, tends to be temperate, the gulf coast intemperately hot and dry most of the year. The nature of these temperature differences is indicated in tables 1.1 and 1.2 and in the accompanying text.

The entire gulf coast is characterized by a summer, rather than a winter, precipitation maximum. Despite this, however, north of San Luis Gonzaga (lat. 29° 49′ N), summer precipitation is so light as to be of little value in promoting plant growth. It doubtless is effective, however, in maintaining plant life, even in the extreme xerophytes that grow there. This effect would appear to be most important during the first year or two of establishment while most of the young root systems are still shallow and inextensive.

South of Bahía de Los Angeles, or about lat. 29° N, the *chubascos* increase the summer average, in September in particular, with the result that the total summer precipitation considerably exceeds that of the winter. Because of high summer temperatures, low relative humidity, and the consequent high evaporation rates, this summer rainfall is less effective than the smaller amounts that fall during the winter. Effectivity is further reduced by the infrequent but highly intensive character of the *chubasco* rains, and the consequent high runoff losses.

The most severe drought of the year throughout the length of the gulf coast occurs during the four-month spring period from March through June. Only rarely does any effective rain fall during this season, which might more properly be designated not as spring but as the foresummer drought period. Although October and November are also dry, occasional rains during these months may temper the aridity, while lower temperatures reduce evapo-transpiration losses somewhat.

Temperature. Despite the few miles that separate the east and west coasts of Baja California, temperature patterns of the two areas are markedly dissimilar. In contrast with the relatively cool summers of the Pacific coast, those of the gulf coast are distinctly hot.

As previously shown in table 1.1, for example, a series of 13 stations along the Pacific coast had a mean annual temperature of 67.6 F. In contrast with this, nine stations along the gulf coast had a mean annual temperature of 74.1 F (table 1.2). The higher gulf coast mean is due to higher temperatures during the spring, summer, and fall, rather than to winter or year round differences.

December, January, and February are the coldest months throughout the gulf coast region, with monthly means of 63, 60, and 62 F respectively. It may be noted that these means are essentially the same as those of the Pacific coast for the same months. Although there is little mean temperature difference anywhere along the gulf between any of these three months, January is consistently somewhat colder than either December or February. Not until one reaches Loreto at lat. 26° N. is there any apparent tendency toward higher mean winter temperatures with progress southward. Here, however, the mean January temperature is 63 F as compared with 59 F at Mulegé approximately 70 miles north. As points of reference, the January average at Tucson, Arizona is 49.6 F, at Yuma 54.6, and at Los Angeles, California 54.2 (U.S. Dept. Agric., 1941). Although not usual, occasional frosts may occur along the coast as far south as Loreto.

Although temperatures tend to be high throughout the six-month period from May through October, July, August, and September are the hottest months. The mean monthly temperatures for the nine stations used in this analysis showed July with an average mean of 87 F, August with 88, and September with 86.

Maximum daily temperatures during the summer months are high along the gulf coast, generally ranging between 100 and 120 F. Night temperatures are also high, usually between 80 and 100 F. Relative humidity along the coast is considerably higher (and so is the discomfort index during the long, hot summer) than it is even a few miles inland.

Interior

Precipitation. The interior of Baja California receives considerably more precipitation than the lower-lying areas of either the Pacific or the gulf coast. Twenty-three interior stations were selected that appeared to give a representative cross-section of the peninsula interior from near the California border to near the southern tip (table 1.3). These stations have a mean annual precipitation of 8.29 inches, about twice that of either coast. The amount that falls is markedly affected by elevations at the highest locations, both in the mountains of the north and the south. Thus, San Juan de Dios, at an elevation of about 4,600 feet in the Sierra San Pedro Mártir, receives about 13 inches, and Sierra de la Laguna, in the south at about 6,800 feet, receives 28.5 inches.

It is a certainty that the San Juan de Dios record does not indicate the full amount of precipitation that falls over extensive portions of the San Pedro Mártir range since the highest peak, Picacho del Diablo, which lies some 30 to 40 miles west of San Felipe, rises to slightly more than 10,000 feet, and an extensive portion of this region lies between 5,000 and 10,000 feet.

In contrast with the northwest Pacific coast, which typically receives no summer rains, the mountainous interior has a summer-winter precipitation regime. The summer rains, which usually fall during July, August, and September, result from the same moisture-laden air from the Gulf of

TABLE 1.3

Precipitation and temperature data for 23 interior Baja California weather stations *

Station	*Years of Record*	*Latitude* (deg. min. sec. N)	*Elevation* (feet)	*Precipitation* (inches)	*Temperature* (mean annual degrees F)
La Rumorosa	24	32-33-00	3,937	5.44	59
San Juan de Dios	10	32-08-00	4,593	13.13	56
Santa Catarina Norte	7	31-40-30	4,068	7.68	59
Valle Trinidad	7	31-19-30	2,953	9.00	61
Rosarito de SPM	9	30-29-30	2,559	4.20	64
San Agustín	10	29-56-30	1,903	3.88	65
Santa Catarina Sur	12	29-43-30	1,476	4.71	66
San Luis	6	29-43-00	1,640	3.88	65
Chapala	12	29-30-30	1,903	3.62	63
Punta Prieta	11	28-58-00	656	3.64	68
San Borja	9	28-47-00	1,230	5.61	68
El Arco	13	28-00-00	984	5.53	69
El Tablón	9	27-37-00	262	4.48	69
San Ignacio	27	27-16-30	344	3.63	71
Comondú	27	26-04-30	853	5.70	73
San Javier	12	25-51-00	1,427	11.74	66
La Poza Honda	14	25-21-00	492	5.61	72
Iraki	8	24-49-30	525	8.46	73
El Pilar	21	24-28-00	410	5.11	74
San Antonio	16	23-48-30	1,230	17.68	74
San Bartolo	25	23-44-00	1,296	12.40	72
San Felipe	18	23-10-30	1,444	17.14	73
Sierra Laguna	15	23-29-30	6,800	28.50	58
Average				8.29	

*Data from Hastings and Humphrey, 1969.

Mexico that brings summer rains to the mainland of Mexico and to southwestern United States. The bulk of this moisture is dropped east of the Gulf of California, largely at relatively high elevations. After crossing the gulf or moving in a northwesterly direction up the peninsula, the warm air, still bearing some moisture, is uplifted and cooled as it encounters the Juarez and San Pedro Mártir mountains. Convection results in additional uplift and cooling with resultant condensation and not infrequent thundershowers, particularly during July and August. As the air masses move on to the northwest and the Pacific they contain little moisture; and as they become warmer with a decrease in elevation, their ability to hold water increases, resulting in the Pacific coast summer aridity.

The summer rainy season is only about half as long as the winter season, and the moisture falls during a period when evaporation rates are relatively high. Nonetheless, at the higher elevations there is enough rain to produce good plant growth. An increase in summer precipitation occurs on the gulf coast at comparable latitudes, but the total along the coast is much less than that of the high mountain areas. As a consequence of this difference in precipitation and much higher gulf coast temperatures, there is typically little or no plant growth during the summer in the low-lying desert areas east of the mountains.

More than half of the precipitation in the interior of the northern portion of the peninsula of Baja California to about as far south as lat. 28° N (the division between the state of Baja California Norte and the territory of Baja California Sur) falls during the winter. South of this parallel more than half comes during the summer (Hastings and Humphrey, ibid.). This summer maximum is due in part to the *chubascos* that usually originate far to the south and move in a general northerly direction.

August is usually the summer month with the heaviest rainfall, although September is almost as wet. The mean monthly precipitation received at the established stations during one or the other of these months ranges from 1.39 inches at Santa Catarina Norte (elevation 4,068 feet, lat. 31° 40′ N) in the Sierra San Pedro Mártir to a minimum of .41 inches at Punta Prieta (elevation 656 feet, lat. 28° 58′ N) and a maximum of 7.4 inches near the southern end of the peninsula at Sierra de la Laguna (elevation ca. 6,800 feet, lat. 23° 30′ N).

There are two periods of drought, spring and fall, throughout the interior, as there also are along the gulf coast and the approximate southern half of the Pacific coast. The spring drought is much more protracted and more severe than that of the fall, lasting for two to three months in the north and about five months in the south. In the north, May and June are typically the driest months, while in the south, February, March, April, May, and June are characteristically dry. During the fall the extreme drought is usually restricted to a relatively short period of one to two months. North of San Ignacio, it is inclined to be about equally severe during both October and November; to the south, occasional late *chubasco* rains may provide moisture in October, thus shortening both the length and severity of the drought.

Temperature. The 18 moderate-elevation interior stations of table 1.3 have an average mean annual temperature of 69 F. It will be noted from the table that with progress southward there is a gradual but rather consistent tendency for the mean annual temperature to increase. The Pacific coast stations show a similar, though less consistent, trend. In contrast, the gulf coast stations exhibit no such tendency.

Temperatures in the high mountains of the north (Sierra Juarez and Sierra San Pedro Mártir) and of the Cape Region in the south (Sierra de la Laguna) average considerably lower than those in the lower-lying area that separates them. Thus, the first four stations of table 1.3 have an average mean annual temperature of 59 F, and the single high-elevation station in the southern mountains has a mean of 58 F.

The official records do not include daily maximum and minimum temperatures, but these vary widely from north to south, from season to season, and from day to night at a given time and location. Summer temperatures in most of the central-interior desert areas tend to be high both day and night. Daily maxima typically range between 85 and 95 F, minima between 75 and 85 F. During the winter the minima, which again usually occur during the night, may typically range between 40 and 60 F at night and 70 to 80 F during the day. Both of these are approximations; they may also be modified by current meteorological conditions, including precipitation accompanying prevailing storm fronts.

2

General Vegetational Characteristics of Baja California

Several publications dealing with certain botanical features of Baja California have served either as a primary basis for the following brief description of the vegetation, or as supplements to my own observations. The publications that have been consulted principally are Shreve and Wiggins' (1964) extensive treatment of the ecology and flora of the Sonoran Desert; the earlier coverage of the entire peninsula by Nelson (1922); the plant records of Goldman (1916) obtained at the time of Nelson's expedition; the land plants of the Allan Hancock Pacific Expeditions as compiled and analyzed by Gentry (1949); the Smithsonian Institution publication on the trees and shrubs of Mexico by Standley (1920–26); and the papers by Brandegee (1892) and Shreve (1937) on the vegetation of the Cape Region.

Historical development

The vegetation of Baja California is the end result of a desert flora that has survived or evolved through millennia of geologic and climatic changes and is adapted to the current environment, including, usually most importantly, climate. Gentry (ibid.) comments on this effect of the geologic history on the biota (p. 85):

> It was inevitable that the evolution of the fauna and flora developed synchronously with the radical physiographic stages . . . Plant populations were repeatedly restricted or provided with new areas and divergent habitats. This affected lines of descent with swamping, with infrequent crossing opportunities, with new placements for variants and chance natural selections, and also with entire eliminations.

Since about the beginning of the Pleistocene epoch when physiographic activities in Baja California appear to have become essentially stabilized, the biota of the peninsula have no longer been subjected to these radical modifying pressures. As a consequence, they presumably have continued to change more slowly under the pressure of gradual migrational tendencies or climatic changes. Even so, during the approximate two to four million years that have since elapsed, there has been time for the occurrence of many evolutionary changes in both the fauna and flora.

Present vegetation

Because of the great diversity of climate encountered in Baja California, one would expect to find a similar variation in its vegetation. This proves to be the case.

Five major vegetation types that are determined primarily by climate may be delineated through the extent of the peninsula. These five are: (1) conifer forest, (2) pine-juniper-oak woodland, (3) chaparral, (4) Sonoran Desert, and (5) catinga. Nelson (ibid.) gave a fairly detailed, well-illustrated account of the vegetation of the entire peninsula, although he did not classify it according to these five categories. His discussion is both readable and reliable, and one interested in a brief but informative discussion of the more common species of both plants and animals should refer to his report.

Conifer forest

The coniferous forest is restricted to the higher elevations of the Sierra Juarez and Sierra San Pedro Mártir above 4,500 feet. The principal coniferous species include Jeffrey pine *(Pinus ponderosa* var. *jeffreyi)* as the major dominant (fig. 2.1), and sugar pine *(P. lambertiana)*, lodgepole pine *(P. contorta),* white fir *(Abies concolor),* and incense cedar *(Libocedrus decurrens)* (Nelson, ibid.). Although these trees may intermingle to some extent, the individual species tend to dominate on specific habitats. They also occur intermixed in varying degrees with a few broad-leaved species. Of these, quaking aspen *(Populus tremuloides)* and canyon oak *(Quercus chrysolepis)* are the most common.

Pine-juniper-oak woodland

This is a woodland of low-growing trees that occurs in the mountains most typically as a zone immediately below the taller conifers but above the chaparral and desert (fig. 2.2). Locally, however, one or more of the woodland trees may occur on the drier sites well within the conifer belt. Three pinyon or nut pines, *Pinus quadrifolia, P. monophylla,* and *P.*

Fig. 2.1. Jeffrey pine in the Sierra Juarez near Laguna Hanson.

Fig. 2.2. Pinyon pine *(Pinus quadrifolia)* in the Sierra Juarez between La Rumorosa and Laguna Hanson.

edulis, occur in the northern mountains; and one, *P. cembroides,* in the highest part of the Sierra Victoria in the Cape Region. One species of juniper *(Juniperus californica)* is widely distributed in both the Juarez and San Pedro Mártir mountains as far south as Cerro El Matomí at about lat. 30° 20′ N. Palmer oak *(Quercus palmeri)* is also a common woodland species of these mountains.

Chaparral

Typical coastal chaparral or, as classified by some botanists, chaparral and coastal sage scrub, extending south from the more extensive stands north of the border in California, occurs along the Pacific coast almost as far south as El Rosario or lat. 30° N. Characteristic hillside and upland shrubs of this chaparral include a wide variety of taxa* including several species of *Ceanothus,* several of *Arctostaphylos,* chamiso *(Adenostoma fasciculatum),* buckeye *(Aesculus parryi),* California sagebrush *(Artemisia californica),* and mountain mahogany, principally *Cercocarpus betuloides* and *C. minutiflorus* (fig. 2.3).

The numerous canyons that cross the chaparral, or that originate in the higher forest or woodland areas, have a more mesic type of vegetation than the adjacent hills. Many of them contain running water at least during the late winter and early spring months and support a semi-riparian type of vegetation including restricted groves of rather large trees. Some of the larger of these trees include California sycamore *(Platanus racemosa)*, coast live oak *(Quercus agrifolia)*, ash *(Fraxinus velutina)*, and Fremont cottonwood or alamo *(Populus fremontii)*. Sagebrush *(Artemisia californica)* and shrubby buckwheat *(Eriogonum fasciculatum)* are common understory shrubs in these drainages.

Sonoran Desert

The Sonoran Desert vegetation, despite its complexity and the extensive area it occupies in Baja California, will be touched on lightly in this chapter. Because representative portions of it are included within the range of the boojum, these will be discussed in some detail later.

Although certain taxa tend to characterize the Sonoran Desert in Baja California, a great deal of variation exists in the relative and actual number of plants from place to place. Under local climatic influence, also, a few species may be so modified as to be hardly recognizable. Of this, more later.

---

*"*Taxon,* plural *taxa,* any botanical taxonomic category, such as the plant kingdom or one of its divisions, classes, orders, families, genera (plural of genus), species, or varieties" (Benson, 1969). For a full discussion of the concept, see Benson, 1962.

Fig. 2.3. Chaparral between Laguna Hanson and La Huerta on the road east from Ensenada.

Although not usually numerically most abundant, certain of the larger forms tend to dominate the landscape in much of the area. This is particularly true with respect to five species, the cirio or boojum *(Idria columnaris);* the cardón cactus *(Pachycereus pringlei);* the elephant tree, *copalquín* or *toróte blanco (Pachycormus discolor);* the maguey or mescal *(Agave shawii);* and the *datilillo (Yucca valida).* Typically growing between these and often much more abundantly are many cacti, most often various species of prickly pear and chollas *(Opuntia* spp.) and *pitáhaya agria (Machaerocereus gummosus).* Finally, but usually the most abundant of all, are several species of bursage, principally *Ambrosia chenopodifolia* and *A. magdalenae.*

The vegetation of much of this desert has a richness and luxuriance that can be fully appreciated only by being seen. The floristic variety that occurs throughout much of the area from north to south and from coast to coast is suggested by a few of the commoner taxa, including two palo verdes *(Cercidium microphyllum* and *Parkinsonia aculeata),* two ocotillos *(Fouquieria splendens* and *F. diguetii),* the boojum or cirio, jojoba *(Simmondsia chinensis), tomatillo (Lycium* spp.), brittlebush *(Encelia farinosa),* mesquite *(Prosopis* spp.), ironwood *(Olneya tesota),* two *copalquíns (Bursera microphylla* and *B. hindsiana), Atamisquea emarginata,* creosotebush *(Larrea tridentata),* and two saltbushes *(Atriplex polycarpa* and

Fig. 2.4. Cape Region low-lying dense thicket of cacti, scrub, and short-stature trees.

A. julacea). Many other species including native palms *(Erythea armata* and *Washingtonia robusta)* occupy specific ecological niches.

Probably no other desert area in the world is as interestingly different as this one. The great variety of plants, large and small, that occur nowhere else and thus that are seen for the first time by the traveler to Baja California, lend an other-world atmosphere to the landscape. On our first visit to this desert, we had the feeling of being in a kind of Alice-in-Wonderland country, a feeling that still persists, several years and many exposures later.

Catinga

This is a close-growing, floristically rich mixture of low-stature trees and tall cacti intermixed with even lower shrubs and cacti. Although the catinga is sometimes referred to as "thorn forest," Shreve (1937) rightly feels that, even if it bears some resemblance to the thorn forest of Sinaloa, it is not dominated by the thorny acacia type of tree and cannot appropriately be designated "thorn forest." His description of the area as resembling an impoverished tropical jungle is apt (fig. 2.4).

The term "catinga" has been adapted from northeastern Brazil where it is used to designate an ecologically similar but floristically different vegetation (Banco do Nordeste do Brasil, 1964). I have employed it here to fill an apparent void in local plant-geographical nomenclature. Shreve's suggested "Cape forest" appears too restrictive because of its geographical implications. "Catinga" can be applied also to the more thorny vegetation of similar appearance and growth form in Sinaloa or elsewhere.

Many of the plants in the Cape (Cabo San Lucas) area were derived originally from the mainland to the east; many others from the desert areas to the north. Shreve (ibid.), in discussing an analysis of the Cape vegetation made some years before, notes than Brandegee (1892) had recorded a total of 732 flowering plants and ferns in the Cape at that time, of which 586 species were restricted to the lowlands, 362 occurred commonly in central and northern Baja California, and 494 were common on the mainland. Four genera and 72 species were believed at that time (1892) to be endemic to the Cape.

The description by Shreve (ibid., p. 110) as quoted below provides a good description of this area:

> The Cape forest below 1,000 meters is distinctly xeric. Its height ranges from 6 to 14 meters (19 to 45 feet), and it varies greatly in density, composition and the growth forms which are represented. Certain areas are dominated by slender leguminous trees and others by stout-stemmed trees with low spreading branches. The canopy of the forest is usually open and always extremely irregular. It is rarely that a single species of tree forms as much as 30% of the stand, except in the case of *Jatropha cinerea*. The low interlacing branches of this tree are an obstacle to progress through the forest. In fact, an open floor is found only in glades along arroyos where *Lysiloma candida*, *L. microphylla* and *Cercidium peninsulare* are dominant. Cacti are almost always omnipresent, *Pachycereus pectenaboriginum* being most abundant where the trees are thickest, and *Lemairocereus thurberi*, *Machaerocereus gummosus* and *Opuntia cholla* most common in the open situations. Shrubs are almost invariably abundant and in slightly moist situations contribute to the formation of impenetrable thickets. One of the commonest shrubs is *Tecoma stans*, which has height and stoutness of stem which almost give it the rank of a tree. Several composite shrubs equal the trees in height and their flowers may be seen projecting from the tallest limbs. The commonest of these are *Viguiera tomentosa*, *V. deltoidea*, *Alvordia fruticosa* and *Eupatorium sagittatum*. The polygonaceous vine *Antigonon leptopus* is abundant in all but the driest situations and its clusters of brilliant crimson flowers do much to give vivid color to a floral display in which yellow is predominant.

3

Where the Boojum Makes Its Home

As will be developed in detail in Chapter 5, the boojum occurs naturally in only one place in the entire world, consisting of two limited portions of the Sonoran Desert in Mexico. The more extensive of these lies in Baja California, the other across the Gulf of California in the state of Sonora. These areas will be referred to here as the *Central Desert* in Baja California and the *Sierra Bacha* in Sonora. Some of their salient geographic and other characteristics are discussed in this chapter.

The Central Desert

The central portion of Baja California contains what may be the most interesting and richest variety of desert plants the world over. This region has been variously called the Vizcaíno Region, the Vizcaíno District, the Vizcaíno Desert Subdistrict, the Vizcaíno Province, the San Borja Desert, and the Central Desert.

The term *Vizcaíno Desert* was apparently first used by E. W. Nelson (1922) because of the adjacent Vizcaíno Bay. As Nelson described the area, the Vizcaíno Desert was restricted to a low-lying Pacific Coastal region characterized largely by low-growing plants (ibid., p. 71):

> A broad and largely sandy plain, which may be called the Vizcaíno Desert, begins on the Pacific coast a little south of Santa Rosalia Bay and extends southeasterly about 150 miles to a point on the coast southeast of Ballenas Bay. On the northern and eastern sides it is limited by the foothills and lower slopes of the great interior plateau. This plain is broadest opposite Scammon Lagoon, where it reaches a width of about 60 miles and narrows to a point at both ends. It is the largest comparatively level area in the peninsula and is excessively arid throughout its extent . . . Near the sea it is mainly flat and sandy, but the shore a few miles north of Santo Domingo Landing is bordered by a belt of high sand dunes replaced inland by a low clay flat, which soon merges into the gradually rising sandy plateau.

Shreve (1951, p. 46) accepts Nelson's terminology and delimitation of the Vizcaíno Desert, describing it as a "coastal plain over 50 km. in length and width . . . at the head of Vizcaíno Bay and [that] extends southeastward toward San Ignacio." The discrepancy in distance between Shreve's 50 km and Nelson's 150 miles seems to have been an accidental misstatement in Shreve's text, as the distance between the points he mentions as the northern and southern limits of the Vizcaíno Desert, and as shown on his map of the Sonoran Desert, is about 100 miles (160 km).

Similarly, Shreve's Vizcaíno Region, of which his Vizcaíno Desert or Plains is a part, is essentially the same as Nelson's Vizcaíno District. According to Shreve (p. 102):

> The Vizcaíno Region comprises the Pacific drainage of central Baja California from the southern end of Sierra San Pedro Mártir south nearly to latitude 26°N. The designation of this subdivision of the Sonoran Desert is an extension of the use of the name "Vizcaíno Desert," which has long been applied to the plains which occupy the long triangular projection. The Vizcaíno Region includes the rough mountainous interior as well as the Vizcaíno Desert and the additional wedge of coastal plain which extends south to Punta Pequeña.

Jaeger (1957) includes a map in which he shows Shreve's (1951) Vizcaíno Region, Magdalena Region, and Central Gulf Coast. The first two of these, however, Jaeger combines as the Vizcaíno-Magdalena Desert. The Vizcaíno Desert of Shreve is referred to by Jaeger as the Vizcaíno Plains. In his 15-page discussion of this area, Jaeger makes no mention of Shreve's monumental work on the Sonoran Desert, which includes the original of the map used by Jaeger and which describes this region in detail.

Johnston (1924) classifies all of the peninsula south of the 30th parallel except for limited southern mountainous areas (his Cape Sierran District) as the Comondú District. This is an extensive area, extending south for roughly 600 miles. Because of its size and latitudinal span, Johnston recognizes that it embraces a considerable variety of conditions and vegetation. He consequently subdivides it into three subdistricts: the Vizcaíno Desert, the Sierra Giganta, and the Cape. His subsequent description indicates that his Vizcaíno Desert Subdistrict is the equivalent of Shreve's Vizcaíno Region (Nelson's Vizcaíno District). None of these areas is shown on either of the two maps that accompany his publication.

Meigs (1966), like Shreve, follows Nelson's original classification of the coastal plain as the Vizcaíno Desert, describing it as a lowland area of five or six thousand square miles.

Aschmann (1959) designates essentially this same central portion of Baja California in part as the Vizcaíno Desert (comparable to the

Vizcaíno Desert of Nelson and of Shreve) and in part as the Central Desert.

Sauer and Meigs (1927) propose the term San Borja Desert for this area, naming it for the 18th Century San Borja Mission located near its center. Aschmann (ibid.) rejects this as implying a limited area and as being a less important location than San Ignacio, which also lies within the Desert boundaries. The same reasoning could logically be applied with reference to Punta Prieta and Guerrero Negro, both of which are established communities within the confines of this area.

Shreve does not mention the Central Desert of Aschmann by any specific geographical name, but it is included as a major part of his Vizcaíno Region. Aschmann also extends his boundaries eastward to the gulf coast, thus including portions of Shreve's Lower Colorado Valley desert and Central Gulf Coast desert.

Both the terminology and geographical limitations of Aschmann's Central Desert are valid phytogeographically. Although less colorful than the other names that might be applied, the term *Central Desert* seems the most appropriate and the least confusing and will be used hereafter in this text (see Map II).

Shreve's designation of the higher-lying portion of the Central Desert as the Sarcophyllous Desert or Agave-Franseria Region is valid up to a point. Both names, however, as with many generalizations, are somewhat misleading. *Agave,* which constitutes one of the dominant genera, *is* sarcophyllous or leaf-succulent. Throughout most of the Region, on the other hand, most of the other dominants, including *Ambrosia (Franseria), Idria, Pachycormus, Pachycereus, Yucca, Viscainoa, Larrea, Machaerocereus, Opuntia, Viguiera,* and *Lycium* are either thin-leaved or stem-succulent.

It might be questioned whether a region as large and complex as the Central Desert can correctly be named for any two genera as, for example, *Agave* and *Ambrosia.* Neither these nor any other two occur throughout, and in many areas where any selected two are found, other species are often more abundant or have a greater ground spread and height.

Whether considered from a point of view of geology, physiography, floristics, or even climate, this is a desert with many faces. Because of its complexity it defies any attempt at simple classification. The various plants that in general characterize it from its northern to its southern and from its eastern to its western boundaries all occupy many ecological niches. Rarely do a majority of the dominant species occur together; each has its particular limitations at some time during its life cycle, so that variations in microhabitats result in varying combinations of species.

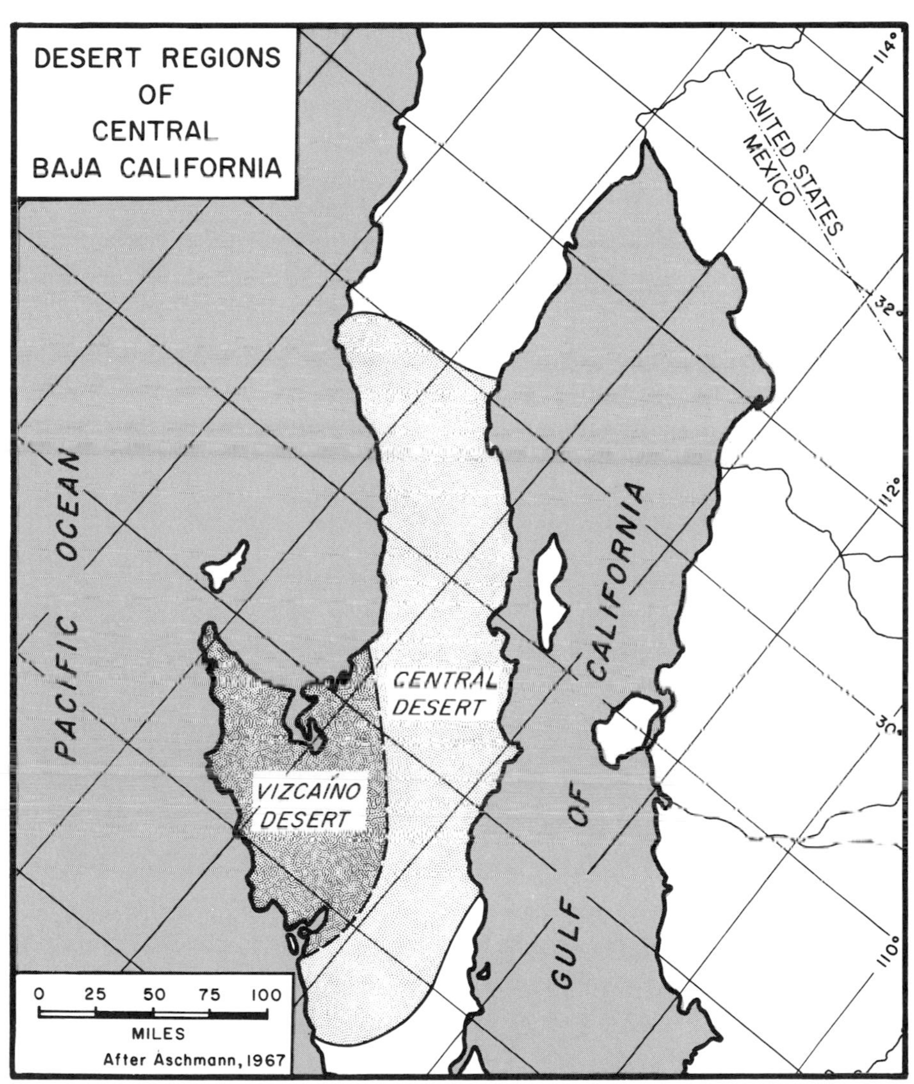
DESERT REGIONS
OF
CENTRAL
BAJA CALIFORNIA
UNITED STATES
MEXICO
114°
32°
112°
30°
110°
PACIFIC OCEAN
GULF OF CALIFORNIA
CENTRAL DESERT
VIZCAINO DESERT
0 25 50 75 100
MILES
After Aschmann, 1967

The Sierra Bacha

The Bacha Mountains, or Sierra Bacha, extend along the coast of Sonora for about 30 miles between Puerto Libertad and Desemboque. The range has a maximum elevation of 2,300 feet and extends inland over most of its extent for about three miles. The constituent rocks cover a thin soil mantle and are largely granite, though with occasional hills of basalt in the southern portion of the range. The bedrock outcrops extensively and is considerably fractured or otherwise weathered, providing a foothold for seedlings of the boojum and other plants.

Except for the limited bajadas at the base of the mountains, there are few gentle slopes in the Sierra Bacha. The abundance of exposed bedrock and surficial residual fragments limits extensive soil losses during the occasional heavy rains. Such vegetation as does occur is mostly open-branched and rather ineffective in the control of erosion.

All of the Sierra Bacha, like all of the Central Desert of Baja California, is classified as Sonoran Desert (Shreve and Wiggins, 1964). Despite the approximately 75 miles of open water that separate the two regions, they have many species in common as well as many that occur only in one location or the other. Concerning this, as well as possible migratory routes, more later.

4

Idria columnaris: Its Name, Phylogeny, and Dim Distant Past

Idria columnaris has long been considered as falling within one of two genera, *Idria* or *Fouquieria.*

The fouquieria family, or Fouquieriaceae, consists at most of only two genera, *Idria* and *Fouquieria,* or, as indicated two paragraphs below, perhaps of only one. If we accept both genera as valid, *Fouquieria* contains up to 10 species depending on the authority accepted; *Idria* consists of the single species, *columnaris.*

There has long been a difference of opinion on this point. Kellogg (1860) in his original description, based on a collection made by Dr. J. A. Veatch in Baja California, called it *Idria.* Curran (1885) and Orcutt (1886), Engler and Melchior (1966), and more recently Henrickson (1972b), have placed it in *Fouquieria.* Nash (1903) in his revision of the family, Standley (1923), and Shreve and Wiggins (1964) recognize it as *Idria.* Shreve, although primarily an ecologist and thus perhaps inclined to accept current taxonomic nomenclature rather than to change it, described the family as containing eight species of *Fouquieria* and the monotypic *Idria* (Shreve, 1931). His publication included a map showing the known distribution of each of the nine species. Shreve's treatment of the family essentially followed that of Standley (ibid.), who in turn had based his work on that of Nash (ibid.). Wiggins (in Shreve and Wiggins, ibid.) listed four species as occurring in the Sonoran Desert.

In his monograph of the Fouquieriaceae, Henrickson (1972b) discusses the family as consisting of 11 species, all belonging to the genus *Fouquieria.* Dr. Henrickson's reasoning in combining the two genera may be of interest primarily to systematic botanists, but is quoted below (Henrickson, 1972a).

I have decided to join *Idria* with *Fouquieria* and the combination I am recognizing for the taxon is *Fouquieria columnaris* (Kellogg) Kellogg ex Curran. . . . The taxon will be the sole member of a newly erected subgenus *Idria* (Kellogg) Henrickson. The other subgenera will be *Bronnia* (H. B. K.) Henrickson for the succulent species *(Fouquieria fasciculata* and *F. purpusii),* and subgenus *Fouquieria* for the woody species. The subgenus *Fouquieria* is divided into two sections, section *Fouquieria* for those with shrubby small-tree habits and section *Ocotilla* Henrickson for the species with an ocotillo habit *(F. splendens,* including *F. campanulata,* and *F. shrevei).*

From my own essentially ecological point of view, the question of nomenclature seems open to debate. Either way, it obviously does not affect the ecology of the plant. For the purposes of this study, therefore, the genus will be referred to as *Idria,* where it was originally placed by Kellogg.

The specific as well as the generic name has been a matter of some difference of opinion, and in the hope that it may at least reduce future confusion, a brief comment is merited here. Kellogg, in his original description, called the species *columnaria,* not *columnaris* (Curran, 1885). This terminology first appeared in a now rather obscure publication, *The Hesperian* (Kellogg, 1960). Despite the initial spelling, the *ia* ending seems to be grammatically in error and as a consequence is untenable. This aspect of the question as analyzed by Henrickson (1972a) follows.

Regarding the ending of the specific epithet of *Fouquieria (Idria) columnaris:* The international rules of Botanical Nomenclature states in Art. 20: The name of a genus is a substantive in the singular number of a word treated as such; and in Art. 23: the specific epithet when adjectival in form and not used as a substantive, agrees grammatically with the generic name. *Fouquieria* or *Idria* are both substantive in the feminine gender, the specific epithet therefore must be feminine singular to be in agreement. [As indicated in] Stearn, Botanical Latin (1966, Hafner Publishing Co.) the adjectival form of columnar is of the group B declension and the ending in the feminine singular nomenclature is *-is;* the *-ia* ending would be used only in the plural, neuter gender. Therefore the *-ia* ending is not in agreement with the gender of the generic name. The ending first used by Kellogg was therefore not correct and would be treated as a grammatical error.

The common names

So far as known, the earliest name for the boojum was *milapá,* used by the Cochimí Indians (Clavijero, 1937). To the Jesuit padres, however, the characteristic appearance of the plant suggested a *cirio,* or taper, the slender type of altar candle used in the Church's religious ceremonies. The earliest reference to this name that has come to my attention is in Wenceslaus Linck's 1762 Report (Burrus, 1967). The Jesuit name of cirio has continued to the present and is the one by which *Idria* is still usually known in Baja California and Sonora, as well as very commonly in the southwestern United States. The name is highly descriptive of many of the plants, and one can readily see why so many who know the plant say, "Why, with an established, descriptive name of this sort, should it be called the boojum?"

The term "boojum" was first applied to it in 1922 by Godfrey Sykes of the Desert Botanical Laboratory in Tucson. Mr. Sykes, who was born and educated in England, was both a scholar and a doer. During his formative years, and doubtless later as well, he had read widely. *The Hunting of the Snark* by Lewis Carroll seems to have been included in his library. In this tongue-in-cheek commentary on many things, Carroll refers to a mythical thing called a "boojum" found in desolate far-off regions.

According to Godfrey's son Glenton, a group of scientists from the Desert Laboratory was standing on an elevated area some distance north of the mountainous area in Sonora where *Idria* had been reported. Godfrey, looking through his telescope and suddenly perceiving the unusual trees, exclaimed "Ho, ho, a boojum, definitely a boojum!" For better or worse, the name stuck and appears destined to persist. It is not inappropriate, and is particularly apt for individuals growing near the Pacific coast of Baja California, that are, even more than most, "like nothing else on earth" (figs. 6.8–6.12, 6.18).

Phylogeny

As indicated by Henrickson (1967), the phylogenetic relationships of the Fouquieriaceae are little known. Henrickson's summary of contributions to a knowledge of the systematic relationships of the family is the most complete to date and is quoted here in full.

Little is known regarding the phylogenetic relationships of the Fouquieriaceae, and its placement in systematic treatments has varied considerably. Initially, Humboldt, Bonpland and Kunth (1823) and Kunth (1824) placed *Fouquieria* in the Portulacaceae. De Candolle in his *Prodromus* (1828) elevated the genus to the family Fouquieriaceae which he associated with the Portulacaceae, but he mentioned similarities with the Crassulaceae, Turneraceae and Loasaceae. Endlicher (1836–1840) and Walpers (1852–1853), treated the group as a subfamily of the Frankeniaceae. Spach (1836) placed the family near the Tamaricaceae, following Bartling's (1830) suggestion. Bentham and Hooker (1862) treated the group as a tribe Fouquieriaceae of the Tamaricaceae. Engler and Prantl (1895) in the first edition of the *Naturlichen Pflanzenfamilien* treated the group as a subfamily Fouquierioideae of the Tamaricaceae. However, in a supplement, Engler (1897) elevated the group to family status Fouquieriaceae, near the Tamaricaceae, a treatment accepted by Hallier (1912) and more recently by Hutchinson (1950), Takhtajan (1954), Cronquist (1957) and others. Bessey (1915) placed the Fouquieriaceae within his Ebenales. Engler (1925) concurred with the opinion of Bessey as did Benson

(1957). In a revision of the family, Nash (1903) urged polemoniaceous affinities. Engler and Gilg (1924), in the tenth edition of the *Syllabus der Pflanzenfamilien,* moved the Fouquieriaceae to the Tubiflorae beside Polemoniaceae. This treatment was also followed in the eleventh and twelfth editions of the *Syllabus der Pflanzenfamilien* (Engler and Diels, 1936: Melchior, 1964) but with reservations. Curiously, the type species of the Fouquieriaceae, *Fouquieria fasciculata,* was first included by Roemer and Schultes (1819) within *Cantua,* a primitive genus of the Polemoniaceae.

Geologic age and evolution

The general appearance of the boojum gives one the feeling that here is a species that has been slow to evolve, that may have changed little for many aeons. And that, if one could have walked in this desert ages ago, he would still have been surrounded by these same familiar trees. Although some of the evidence seems to bear this out, it should be noted that these "conclusions" are based on intuitive reasoning and that there is no confirmed evidence as to the actual age, either of the boojum or of the other members of the family.

Conditions for preservation of plant fossils under desert conditions are notoriously poor. Consequently, fossil evidence showing the composition of desert floras in past geologic ages is usually weak or lacking. Such is the case with *Idria;* there are no known records of fossilized pollen, or, for that matter, of any other portion of the plant.

Axelrod (1952, 1958, 1960) has postulated that *Idria* is descended from a relict derived from a basic tropical antecedent that had become preadapted to a cooler and drier region adjacent to the tropics. He suggests that this occurred early in the evolutionary development of flowering plants during the Permo-Triassic epoch some 200 million years ago in southwestern North America, probably in the area that is now northwestern Mexico. "Although it cannot be demonstrated that such plants as *Pachycereus, Dideria, Pachypodium, Idria,* and others are relict, bradytelic [slow to evolve] plants of the early Mesozoic, the probability is high that they represent their descendants" (ibid., 1960).

It would seem that if *Idria* were descended from some Permo-Triassic ancestor, some form of it could have persisted in essentially its present location during the approximate 115 to 125 million years that have elapsed since the middle Cretaceous. Durham and Allison (1960) have concluded that "great areas on the west side of the Peninsular ranges scarcely have been disturbed since the mid-Cretaceous orogeny," and that despite changes in the coastline the peninsula has persisted since that time.

Gentry (1949) has suggested that despite many and sometimes drastic changes in the shorelines of what is today the peninsula of Baja

California, extensive portions of this area as well as of the mainland to the east may have had a desert climate that has persisted since the middle Mesozoic. If this is so, it may be that the boojum has persisted from its ancestral to its present form under a climate to which it was initially well-enough adapted to have reproduced and has continued with comparatively few changes for the 100 million or so years since the middle Mesozoic.

If, as seems possible, *Idria* does indeed represent a slow-to-evolve plant, this may be explained in part by its slow growth rate. The plants develop very slowly, so that many years, perhaps as much as 50 to 100, may elapse between germination and first flowering. To this add the relatively few years when climatic conditions may permit seedling survival and establishment, and we have a combination of circumstances providing little reproductive opportunity for rapid evolutionary change.

Intuition has been said to be an understanding or depth of perception gained from intimate study of a subject. After studying and thinking about *Idria* off and on for more than 40 years and working and living with it closely for the last five, I have developed a sort of intuitive feeling about many aspects of its existence and development. It appears, for example, to be a plant with a primitive type of branching. The main trunk consists of a single stem more often than of two or more, and, in those instances when it may even develop several, these are simple and seem to occur accidentally rather than as a characteristic feature of the plant.

Branching often appears to be of the simple or primitive dichotomous variety in which a single stem apparently splits and continues growth as two of equal age. The side branches, with their quite different appearance and morphological characteristics, appear to have evolved as a kind of afterthought. It is as though more leaves were needed than could be grown on the main trunk, so just enough and just long enough side branches developed to provide a support for these leaves. The shortness of these branches would seem to have survival value in that they offer little resistance to the winds that otherwise might break off the main trunk.

The water-storage ability of the trunk may represent a modification from a more woody, nonsucculent, or at least less succulent, ancestral type. Although no evidence in support of this has been uncovered in the study, it is proposed here as conforming to the usually accepted concept of the development of this kind of xeromorphism.

All the parts of an organism do not necessarily evolve at equal rates, and so it appears to be with the boojum. Anatomically, the leaves seem to be as advanced as those of the average mesophyte. Despite the fact that they are shed at the first intimation of drought, they have evolved to some extent along xeromorphic lines and possess certain characteristics typical of the leaves of xerophytes (Humphrey, 1935; Henrickson, 1972b).

The habit that the cirio and other members of the family have of shedding their leaves at the first suggestion of drought would seem to be an advanced characteristic that has evolved in response to an arid environment. Although certainly not unique as a means of conserving moisture among desert plants, this adaptation would seem to be more efficient than most changes in shape or size of leaves, or the cutinization that is typical of many xerophytes. Although less efficient than the absence of leaves as in most cacti, the leaves of the boojum apparently persist only as long as there is no water deficit or at most a very slight one.

The floral structure of the boojum throws little light on its evolutionary history. In general, the characteristics of the petals, sepals, stamens, and carpels tend to suggest a somewhat advanced, rather than a primitive, type of flower.

We are left, thus, with various conflicting bits of evidence, some suggesting a primitive, slowly evolving plant and some a plant that is, at least in part, not primitive. With reference to its geologic age, one can only theorize at this point, but, until some sound evidence is found to the contrary, I shall incline to the view that it is the current end of the line for a slow-to-evolve, generally primitive, and geologically very old prototype.

5

Geographic Distribution: Where and, In Part, Why

Idria occurs naturally only in one region of the world, the Central Desert of Baja California and one small range of mountains adjacent to the Gulf of California 75 miles to the east in the state of Sonora (Map III). It is thus restricted not only to the Sonoran Desert, but to a limited portion of that desert.

Baja California distribution

The Baja California population of boojums occurs somewhat discontinuously over an area that extends from northwest to southeast for about 250 miles and from east to west for more than 75 miles. As one travels south from either Tijuana or Mexicali these odd-looking plants are first seen a few miles south of El Rosario, some 200 miles from the border. Few travelers will encounter them south of the general Calmallí to El Arco area because of their restriction to mountainous regions not accessible by car.

The most northwestern location in which we have recorded the boojum is three miles from the Pacific, due west of El Socorro. Here a single mature individual about ten feet tall may be seen outlined against the sky about 100 yards south of the La Suerte road. No others apparently occur in the vicinity. Further inland, we have noted several isolated colonies near the road from El Socorro to Rancho Nuevo and La Suerte. The most northerly of these was at approximate lat. 30° 30′ N, in an area 30 miles from the Pacific at an elevation of 2,100 feet. Two ranchers whom we met there in the summer of 1971 assured us that there were no cirios further inland or further north. As a consequence, we have not looked for them beyond Rosarito de SPM, a ghost town 40 miles from the Pacific. No boojums occurred there, nor were any visible with an eight-power glass. Lack of time and/or the quality or lack of roads have also

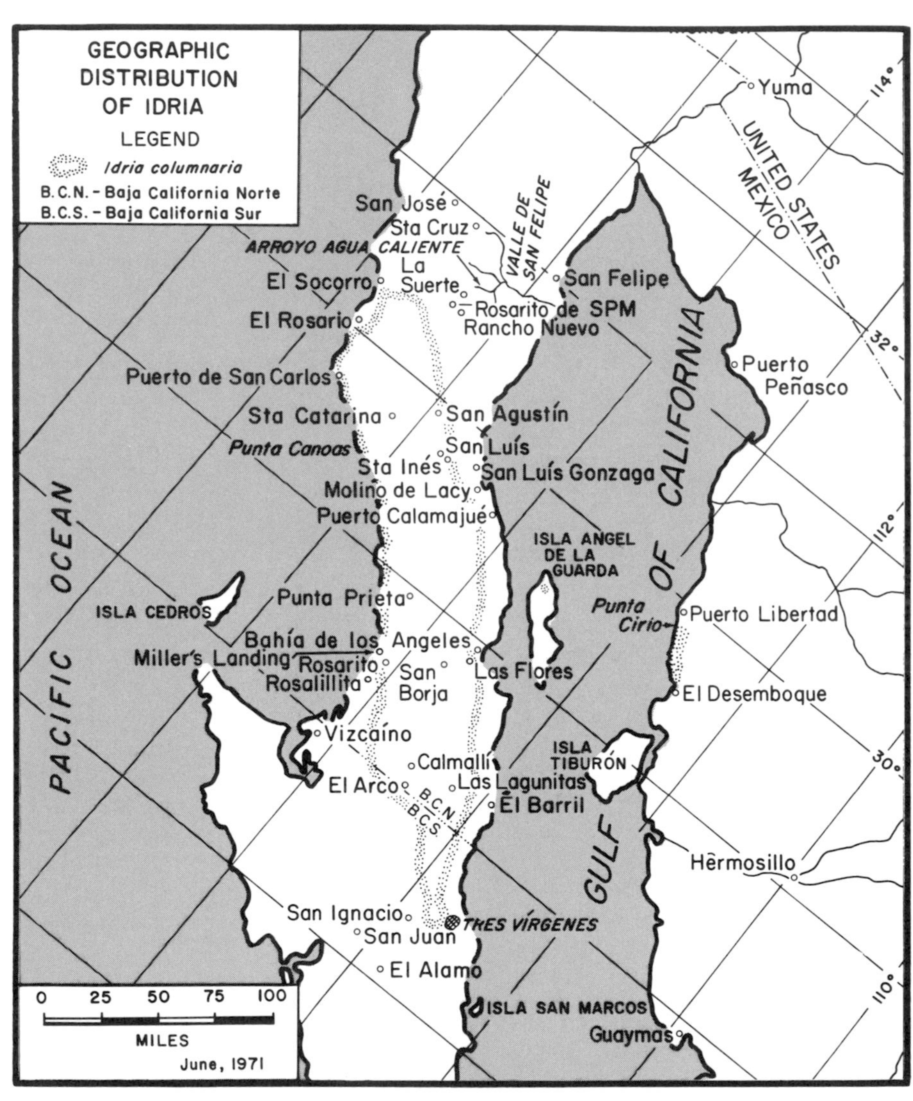
GEOGRAPHIC DISTRIBUTION OF IDRIA
LEGEND
Idria columnaria
B.C.N. - Baja California Norte
B.C.S. - Baja California Sur
Yuma
UNITED STATES
MEXICO
114°
San José
Sta Cruz
VALLE DE SAN FELIPE
ARROYO AGUA CALIENTE
La Suerte
El Socorro
San Felipe
El Rosario
Rosarito de SPM
Rancho Nuevo
32°
Puerto Peñasco
Puerto de San Carlos
Sta Catarina
San Agustín
Punta Canoas
San Luís
Sta Inés
San Luís Gonzaga
Molino de Lacy
Puerto Calamajué
GULF OF CALIFORNIA
112°
PACIFIC OCEAN
ISLA ANGEL DE LA GUARDA
Punta Prieta
Punta Cirio
Puerto Libertad
ISLA CEDROS
Bahía de los Angeles
Miller's Landing
Rosarito
Las Flores
San Borja
Rosalillita
El Desemboque
Vizcaíno
ISLA TIBURÓN
30°
Calmallí
El Arco
Las Lagunitas
BCN
BCS
El Barril
Hermosillo
San Ignacio
TRES VÍRGENES
San Juan
El Alamo
110°
0 25 50 75 100
MILES
June, 1971
ISLA SAN MARCOS
Guaymas

prevented our further exploration into the lower reaches of the Sierra San Pedro Mártir. Earlier, however, we had driven the length of the road west of San Felipe in the Valle de San Felipe to its end south of Arroyo Agua Caliente, studying the eastern slopes of the Sierra San Pedro Mártir with a 60-power spotting scope. Although the search revealed no boojums on any of the slopes or ridges, this does not entirely rule out the possibility of their occurring as isolated colonies in that region.

The southernmost occurrence is on the upper slopes of the Tres Vírgenes volcanic peaks. Here the boojums grow on about the upper third of the peaks in isolated groups or singly, and on all exposures. Close flying in a small plane over the rugged terrain south of here in 1971 revealed not a single individual. There would seem to be no doubt that Tres Vírgenes represents the extreme southern extension of their geographic range.

On the Pacific slope, the boojum occurs occasionally to within a stone's throw (literally) of the coast. Individuals growing this close to the ocean are widely scattered, only rarely being found in any abundance less than about a mile from the shore. The occasional groups that may be seen even this distance inland are limited in number and typically occur on east-facing slopes that receive some protection from the cold winds of the Pacific. Not until one gets about five miles or more from the coast does the species become widespread and occur abundantly on exposed, comparatively level sites.

We have recorded *Idria* near the Pacific coast at a variety of locations extending from a point two miles east of El Socorro to about three miles south of Rosalillita. It occurs intermittently at many locations along the coastal routes from El Rosario to Puerto de San Carlos and from Punta Canoas to Rosalillita, usually approaching the coast most closely where the slopes of the major arroyos provide some protection from the Pacific climate.

On the gulf side of the peninsula, at no point does the cirio approach the water as closely as it does on the Pacific. On the road to Bahía de los Angeles it may be seen about ten miles from the shore and about 800 feet above sea level. As shown on Map III, a few individuals also grow on the north end of Isla Angel de la Guarda. These occur at an elevation of about 4,300 feet.

Most of the gulf coast within the north-south range of *Idria* cannot be reached by car and must be examined from the air or by boat. Along the available roads there are no boojums anywhere in the Molino de Lacy area, nor can any be seen from the road down the canyon to Puerto Calamajué. On the road to El Barril, its nearest approach to the coast is in the hills near Las Lagunitas about 15 miles from the coast and roughly 2,000 feet above sea level.

Sonoran mainland distribution

On the coast of Sonora, *Idria* occurs in about a 30-mile stretch of a coastal mountain range, the Sierra Bacha, that extends from a point six miles south of Puerto Libertad south almost to Desemboque (Map III). Only in one area of these mountains is it found more than about two miles from the coast, even though the mountain mass extends inland some six to eight miles at some places. At the extreme southern end of its range, *Idria* occurs abundantly about 3.5 miles from the shore. So far as known, there is none either to the north, south, or east of the Sierra Bacha, or on nearby Tiburón Island (Isla Tiburón on Map III).

Discussion

Either one of two apparently plausible explanations could account for the present disjunct populations of *Idria* in Baja California and on the mainland of Sonora. The mainland colony could represent a marginal relict of the time some four million years ago when the peninsula lay adjacent to the mainland, or it could have developed from seed blown across the gulf during a tropical hurricane ages ago. Which of these two alternatives is the correct one will probably never be known with certainty. Either could explain the origin of the population in Sonora.

If *Idria* or its prototype dates back to the early Mesozoic (ca. 200 million years ago) as suggested by Axelrod (1960) or even to some much later time, some form of the modern genus undoubtedly was growing in the area that has presumably pulled away from the mainland during the last four million years to become the peninsula of Baja California (Larson, Menard & Smith, 1968; Moore & Buffington, 1968). And, if Gentry (1949) is correct in postulating that extensive portions both of the peninsula and of the mainland to the east have had a persistent desert climate from the mid-Mesozoic to the present, climatic conditions would appear to have favored maintenance of the plant in more or less its present range for at least 100 million years. Certainly it would seem that by the four million years ago birth of the peninsula, *Idria* or its prototype was established and flourishing. This should not be taken to imply that at those times its distribution, either on the peninsula or the mainland, coincided exactly with that of today. Even if the plants were best adapted to essentially the same climatic conditions that most favor them today, they could have extended further north or south than at present.

Were the species highly adaptive and genetically flexible, either through aggressive invasion or development of adaptive races, it should have spread to adjacent areas. Possessing neither of these characteristics, however, its range has been restricted not only in Baja California but even more so on the coast of Sonora. Unlike such wanderers as the ubiquitous tumbleweed *(Salsola kali),* filaree *(Erodium cicutarium),* or puncture weed *(Tribulus terrestris),* the boojum is not a migrant and seems destined never to move far from the highly specialized bit of desert to which it has become adjusted.

The historical geology of the gulf region since the Pliocene supports the theory that the Sonoran boojum population resulted from windblown seeds, rather than being a relict of a former continuous or near-continuous stand extending from the peninsula to the mainland. If, for example, the peninsula of Baja California has gradually been "rafted" away from the mainland during the last four million years, a movement that has also shifted it northward some 170 miles, why do we not find the boojum on the mainland, not only opposite much of its present peninsular range, but even 170 miles to the south? Accepting this northward and westward continental drift, why is there no *Idria* on the peninsula today within at least 150 miles from that portion of it that presumably lay adjacent to the mainland *Idria* stand of today? This would have placed it near the head of the Gulf and in the lower Colorado River drainage, an area so dry that few of the Central Desert species occur there today. Perhaps there has been a long-continued, gradual change toward a drier climate as the peninsula has shifted toward the northwest, resulting in a concomitant shift of most of the plant species southward. A few plants such as creosotebush, bursage *(Ambrosia dumosa),* brittlebush *(Encelia farinosa),* and ironwood that apparently have been able to adjust to the increase in aridity, have persisted and occur there today, although usually as widely scattered individuals.

This line of reasoning brings us back to the probability of establishment of the stand from seeds blown across the gulf at some far distant time, perhaps only tens or at most hundreds of thousands of years ago. The boojum produces large quantities of wind-disseminated seeds (fig. 5.1) during the latter part of the *chubasco* or hurricane season. These storms are usually featured by winds of high velocity blowing from south to north and northeast. The incidence of *chubascos* is sufficiently high that there would seem to have been many opportunities when seeds might have been carried across the gulf in numbers large enough to seed favorable coastal areas. Hastings and Turner (1965), in their analysis of the climate of Baja California, cite records indicating that an average of one tropical cyclone of tropical storm intensity or greater might be expected to strike the peninsula each year, and that one out of two of these would reach hurricane intensity. That there must have been many thousands of such high intensity hurricanes sweeping through this area since the birth of the boojum, many of them blowing from the peninsula to the mainland, seems beyond question. It would appear to be almost a certainty that not only once, but many times, seeds not only of *Idria* but of other species as well must have been carried across the approximate 75-mile stretch of open water and dropped on the mainland.

Seeds in large numbers falling in a favorable habitat at a time of excessive rainfall certainly could account for the mainland colony. And

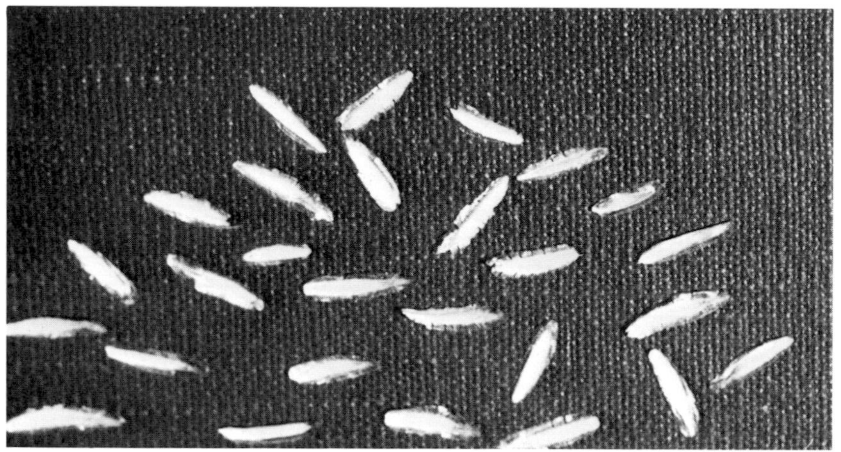

Fig. 5.1. Typical *Idria* seeds, about 15 mm in length. Note the small, peripheral "wing" that aids in dissemination of the seeds by wind.

it is not only possible, but even highly probable, that the same combination of fortuitous circumstances could have occurred not once but many times.

It has not been possible in the present study to undertake a sufficiently detailed analysis of all the evidence to propose a single definite answer to the riddle of the origin of the mainland boojums. A statistical evaluation of the principal taxa, both plant and animal, that are common to the peninsula and to at least that portion of the mainland where *Idria* grows today should prove invaluable in such an analysis. Aside from this, however, the Sierra Bacha area appears to represent a marginal habitat where establishment is difficult.

Distribution in relation to climate

General aspects

The distribution of *Idria* in relation to precipitation and temperature was analyzed principally by an evaluation of the records of 18 Mexican Government weather stations in Baja California and three in Sonora (Hastings, 1964; Hastings & Humphrey, 1969a,b). Six of the Baja California stations were located in the interior of the peninsula where the boojum is most abundant and achieves its best development, three were in the interior adjacent to but north of its range, three were in the interior adjacent to but south of its range, three were on the Pacific coast within its latitudinal range, and three were on the gulf coast where there was no *Idria* but within its latitudinal range. Two of the Sonoran stations were located on the gulf coast, one about six miles north of the boojum stand there, the other an equal distance south of the stand. The third lay about 100 miles to the northwest.

Analysis of the climatic data from weather stations both within and without the range of *Idria* indicates that its geographic distribution is correlated with various aspects of climate; principally annual and seasonal amount and distribution of precipitation and their variability from year to year, minimum and maximum temperature means and extremes, and relative humidity. In addition, local distribution is at times determined by microclimate resulting from insolation and proximity to the Pacific Ocean or the Gulf of California and consequent relative humidity and exposure to prevailing winds.

Concepts of season

The yearlong climate, both within the range of *Idria* and in the adjacent areas, can be, and sometimes is, divided into four equal-length seasons (Hastings & Humphrey, 1969a). Such a breakdown, while it simplifies statistical calculations, often does not coincide with the growing seasons, or with phenological changes in the vegetation. In order for a season to have biological meaning and be useful in explaining the life and death processes of plants and animals, its principal components such as temperature and precipitation should be consistently similar. These periods of similarity may or may not be identical with calendar seasons. Nor may the months that characterize a season in one area necessarily be identical with those for the same season in an adjacent area.

Any seasonal breakdown is limited with respect to application by the kinds of data available and the periods for which these have been summarized. Thus, in the present instance, the data include precipitation and temperature expressed as monthly totals and means, respectively, and as annual totals and means. There are no records for wind velocity, relative humidity, cloud cover, evaporation rates, or the incidence of fog, nor do the available statistics show daily conditions; so that in no instance have I been able to use a different period of time than the standard calendar month. Despite these limitations, it has been possible to relate plant developmental processes rather satisfactorily to climate through a flexible concept of seasons, as below.

Peninsular interior within Idria*'s range*

In my analysis of climatic conditions, five seasons which, while essentially distinct, do grade into each other, have been distinguished for the *Idria*-supporting interior Central Desert region of Baja California. These seasons are: (1) the winter rains (December, January, February); (2) the spring drought (March, April); (3) the arid foresummer (May, June, July); (4) the summer rains (August, September); and (5) the fall drought (October, November).

Effective precipitation during any year in Baja California, as well as in that portion of Sonora where the boojum occurs, is uncertain at best and lacking at worst. In both areas, however, it is characterized by a pattern of summer-winter rains and spring-fall drought. This bimodal precipitation regime is believed to be essential to establishment and survival of the young boojum plants in all of Baja California where they occur, except for a restricted Pacific coastal strip, as well as for the single population in Sonora. The need for this "dual stimulation" was suggested as a possibility by Aschmann (1959, p. 11).

Although germination and initial establishment may be restricted to the winter and early spring, the plants probably can survive the heat of summer (except in a limited portion of the Pacific coast) only in those areas that characteristically receive an essential minimum of summer rain, combined with a survivable temperature range. This combination of precipitation and temperature is shown in table 5.1 for six Baja California weather stations. Note that December, January, and February are the "wet" months, with March and April becoming progressively drier. Temperatures are at their monthly minima during the winter period, thus creating a potentially favorable precipitation-evaporation ratio.

The arid foresummer months of May, June, and July are either entirely or almost dry at a time when temperatures are rising and most plants cease growing and, as with *Idria* and *Pachycormus,* shed their leaves.

The critically essential summer rains fall most commonly in August and September before the onset of the moderately severe fall drought. It is these rains which, slight though they may be, seem to make the difference between life and death for the young boojums. In this connection

TABLE 5.1

Mean monthly precipitation and temperature data for 6 interior Baja California weather stations*

Station	*Years of Record*	*Precip. (in) Temp. (F)*	*Jan*	*Feb*	*Mar*	*Apr*	*May*	*Jun*	*Jul*	*Aug*	*Sep*	*Oct*	*Nov*	*Dec*	*Annual*
San Agustín	10	P	76	.33	.41	.09	.00	.00	.00	.19	.79	.24	.17	.87	3.85
		T	52	55	56	62	65	72	79	79	76	77	59	54	65
Sta. Catarina	12	P	.91	.62	.49	.20	.00	.00	.02	.13	.44	.30	.37	1.17	4.65
		T	55	56	59	62	66	71	79	80	77	70	63	59	66
San Luis	6	P	.63	.21	.20	.19	.00	.00	.07	.34	.69	.17	.21	1.18	3.89
		T	55	56	57	61	65	59	79	80	75	69	61	55	65
Punta Prieta	11	P	.62	.43	29	.11	.00	.00	.04	.41	.27	.34	.24	.88	3.63
		T	59	60	62	64	68	72	78	80	77	71	64	61	68
San Borja	9	P	.76	.66	.42	.13	.01	.00	.15	.71	.76	.10	.23	1.69	5.62
		T	59	60	62	65	66	71	77	79	77	72	67	61	68
Rosarito	8	P	.58	.63	19	.12	.00	.00	.04	.23	.80	.24	.66	1.49	4.98
		T	59	59	60	62	63	65	73	75	75	71	65	60	66
Average		P	.71	.48	.33	.14	.00	.00	.05	.34	.63	.23	.31	1.21	4.44
		T	57	58	59	63	66	70	78	79	76	72	63	58	67

*Data from Hastings and Humphrey, 1969a.

it should be kept in mind that the data included in table 5.1, as in the other tables in this section, show only monthly and annual means for the entire period of record; they do not indicate conditions prevailing during any specific year. If the precipitation received during any month never exceeded these average figures it is highly doubtful whether either the boojums or much of the other vegetation would ever become established. Favorable conditions probably occur infrequently between intervals of many years with no establishment. These exceptional years would be characterized by an unusually cool, moist winter and spring, followed the same year by a summer of much heavier than average rains. This is indicated by the fewness of boojum seedlings, as well as by a tendency for the plants to fall into rather definite height classes in specific areas.

The ten-year record at San Borja shows only one year, 1965–66, when suitable germination and establishment conditions of these sorts may have prevailed. In December 1965 precipitation was four times the average (6.9″ vs 1.7″); January was about 1.5 times the average (1.26″ vs .76″); and February was slightly more than twice normal (1.40″ vs .65″). That summer, although August was relatively dry (.20″ as compared with an average .71″), September received almost four times the long-time average (2.95″ vs .76″) and October had six times its average (.63″ vs .10″). None of the other six interior stations included in the analysis showed so marked a series of sequential winter-summer months that might have favored both germination and establishment.

The brevity of the period of record prevents determination of the long-time frequency of occurrence of favorable years. Limited as the data are, however, they do tend to bear out the conclusion, already tentatively reached from field observations, that young boojums do not become established every year despite a usually abundant seed crop. The study has not continued long enough to determine how often conditions are conducive to establishment of enough seedlings to maintain most stands, but it is questionable whether these conditions prevail oftener than about once in ten years. The longevity of the plants and the few dead ones that are usually seen even in moderately dense stands suggest that even this figure may be too conservative, and that it may not be unreasonable to assume even a 15- or 20-year establishment interval.

Peninsular interior north of Idria*'s range*

The interior immediately north of *Idria*'s range has seasonal precipitation characteristics distinctly different from most of the Central Desert (table 5.2). The winter rainy season is more prolonged in the north, the rains falling during the four months from November through February and continuing, though in lesser amounts, through March and April. This relatively long wet season is followed by an extremely dry foresummer extending from May through July, and this in turn by an additional three months of continued but slightly less arid conditions before the onset of the winter rains in November. Fundamentally, therefore, this region has two distinct and extended seasons; six months of winter rains and six months of summer drought. In this, it resembles the Pacific Coastal area adjoining it on the west.

The northward distribution of the boojum in the interior of the peninsula may be limited in part by a deficiency of summer precipitation and in part by low winter temperatures. Although the mean annual precipitation of the stations used in this analysis is higher adjacent to but north of the boojum's range than within the range (6.88″ and 4.44″ respectively), summer rains during July, August, and September for these "outside" stations total .83″ as contrasted with 1.02″ within the range (tables 5.2, 5.1). Even this slight difference may be critical, and, despite the higher winter precipitation "outside," it is highly possible that the plants cannot survive the long summer drought which extends through the six hottest months of the year from May through October. Only extreme xerophytes well-adjusted to a single season of precipitation can persist here, where there is no effective precipitation for so many months during the summer heat.

The records do not include temperature extremes. This is unfortunate, particularly in the case of minima that might determine the upper altitudinal and northern limits, not only of *Idria,* but of other desert species as well.

At the observed upper and northern limits of the boojum it was growing intermixed with some California juniper. The occurrence of juniper, although not necessarily correlated with winter temperatures that might restrict the boojum, is suggestive of this. The elevation (2,100′) and the distance from the tempering effect of the Pacific (30 miles) provide additional support for the possibility of lethal freezing temperatures.

Although *Idria* will survive when exposed to much lower temperatures than are usual within its range, the occurrence of subfreezing conditions near its upper altitudinal limits may be a factor that kills some seedlings, and combined with aridity, determines its ultimate upward or northern limits in the interior.

Peninsular interior immediately south of Idria*'s range*

Although, as indicated in table 5.3, the interior Central Desert immediately south of the boojum's range is more arid than that portion within its range, the seasons in the two regions are rather similar. In both instances five seasons can be distinctly defined. However, the winter

TABLE 5.2

Mean monthly precipitation and temperature data for 3 interior Baja California weather stations adjacent to the distribution of *Idria* on the north*

Station	*Years of Record*	*Precip. (in) Temp. (F)*	*Jan*	*Feb*	*Mar*	*Apr*	*May*	*Jun*	*Jul*	*Aug*	*Sep*	*Oct*	*Nov*	*Dec*	*Annual*
San José	7	P	1.31	1.76	.64	.43	.00	.05	.06	.13	.34	.39	1.07	1.64	7.82
		T	49	50	52	57	59	67	74	75	70	64	57	51	60
Sta. Cruz	7	P	1.19	.70	.89	.62	.00	.03	.20	.51	.58	.59	1.48	1.85	8.64
		T	46	47	49	53	55	60	69	66	63	59	53	49	56
Rosarita de SPM	9	P	.74	.70	.45	.31	.00	.00	.07	.41	.19	.23	.40	.71	4.21
		T	56	59	59	63	64	67	70	71	69	66	61	60	64
Average		P	1.08	1.05	.66	.45	.00	.03	.11	.35	.37	.40	.98	1.40	6.89
		T	50	52	53	58	59	65	71	71	67	63	57	53	60

*Data from Hastings and Humphrey, 1969a.

TABLE 5.3

Mean monthly precipitation and temperature data for 3 interior Baja California weather stations adjacent to the distribution of *Idria* on the south*

Station	*Years of Record*	*Precip. (in) Temp. (F)*	*Jan*	*Feb*	*Mar*	*Apr*	*May*	*Jun*	*Jul*	*Aug*	*Sep*	*Oct*	*Nov*	*Dec*	*Annual*
San Ignacio	27	P	.40	.27	.35	.00	.00	.00	.28	.64	.84	.28	.21	.37	3.64
		T	61	62	65	68	71	76	82	83	82	75	68	63	71
El Álamo	17	P	.46	.13	.19	.00	.00	.00	.07	.60	.38	.21	.07	.67	2.78
		T	62	62	65	68	71	76	82	85	82	75	67	65	72
San Juan	8	P	.52	.21	.00	.00	.00	.00	.10	.20	.15	.26	.06	.40	1.90
		T	63	63	64	69	70	73	81	84	82	76	75	64	72
Average		P	.46	.20	.18	.00	.00	.00	.15	.48	.46	.25	.11	.48	2.77
		T	62	62	65	68	71	75	82	84	82	75	70	64	72

*Data from Hastings and Humphrey, 1969a.

rains in the southern area, in addition to being markedly less for each month in which they fall, are restricted essentially to the two months of December and January. The early spring months of February and March are essentially dry, rarely receiving any effective rainfall. The foresummer months of April, May, and June are totally dry. July, August, and September make up the relatively wet summer, while October and November become progressively drier.

The available data on precipitation and temperature suggest that the southern limits of *Idria*'s distribution are probably determined by increasing aridity. The three interior stations selected as typical of conditions adjacent to its distribution on the south, for example, have a mean annual precipitation of 2.77″ as contrasted with 4.44″ for the six interior stations to the north. In addition, the mean annual temperatures for these groups of stations are 72 F and 67 F, respectively. Although the summer months to the south are slightly less arid than those to the north, the critical moisture deficiency apparently occurs during the important winter months. Within the boojum's range, for example, December, January, and February have a total rainfall of 2.40″, while these same months to the south record less than half as much, or only 1.14″. Summer temperatures during July, August, and September average 5 F higher to the south, thus reducing the effectiveness of the summer rains.

Pacific coast

The Pacific coast, both within and north of *Idria*'s range, has a single two-season pattern of winter rain and summer drought. The winter rains extend through December, January, and February, decreasing rapidly during March and April. The four summer months from May through August are almost totally dry. The fall months of September, October, and November show a slight increase in precipitation, but effective rains rarely fall again until December.

I have not been able to explain the complete absence of *Idria* on the Pacific coast north of El Rosario and El Socorro on a basis of any of the available climatic data. Neither precipitation nor temperature would seem to differ sufficiently north of El Rosario and El Socorro along the Pacific from the area to the south within *Idria*'s range to prevent establishment of at least an occasional individual north of the present known range. This entire coastal region is subjected to year-long cool, moisture-laden winds blowing off the cold waters of the Pacific. Much of the year there is a night and morning fog that further compensates in part for a low precipitation level.

There are only three weather stations near the Pacific from El Socorro to Vizcaíno, a distance of about 200 miles, consequently the climatic picture for this area is sketchy at best. The available data, as summarized in table 5.4, indicate a long, dry summer and a single season of precipitation during the winter throughout this coastal area. The periods of record (11 years at El Socorro, 14 at El Rosario, and 10 at Vizcaíno), are too short to provide mean monthly statistics of the desired reliability, but are the only ones available. The Vizcaíno record, although showing heavier rainfall in September than during any other month except December, probably does not accurately portray the typical September precipitation for that region. September, like the entire nine-month period from March through October, is usually dry, and the apparent September increase is due to an abnormal 5.5″ that fell in 1966, probably largely during a single *chubasco*.

The seasonal precipitation and temperature patterns for El Rosario and El Socorro are typical also of the Pacific coastal stations of the peninsula north of the range of *Idria*. In view of the similarity of both precipitation and temperature within and without the range, it would seem either that the climatic record does not include certain critical characteristics restrictive to *Idria* or that one or more factors other than climate are involved.

South of El Rosario, the few boojums that become established near the coast probably reflect the abundant seed source adjacent to the east. North of El Rosario and El Socorro there is no reliable seed source available. Inasmuch as the Pacific climate is at best poorly suited for the establishment, not only of the boojum but indeed for most of the interior Central Desert vegetation, it seems logical to suggest that the growth of *Idria* north of its present distribution along the Pacific is prevented by the combination of an unfavorable climate and the fewness or complete lack of seeds.

Gulf coast east of Idria*'s range*

The gulf coast east of *Idria*'s range, because of its greater aridity, has a less complicated seasonal pattern than the interior. Thus, there is a three-month winter rainy season (December-February), a four-month late spring and foresummer drought (March-June), three months of summer rains (July-September), and a two-month fall drought (October-November).

The boojum is apparently unable to become established adjacent to the gulf coast because of the consistently higher temperatures and lower precipitation there than in the interior. Mean monthly temperatures for three representative gulf coast stations average 73.6 F as compared with 66.5 F for six interior stations (tables 5.5, 5.1). Not only did the coastal temperatures average seven degrees higher than those of

TABLE 5.4

Mean monthly precipitation and temperature data for 3 Pacific coast, Baja California, weather stations within the latitudinal distribution of *Idria**

Station	*Years of Record*	*Precip. (in) Temp. (F)*	*Jan*	*Feb*	*Mar*	*Apr*	*May*	*Jun*	*Jul*	*Aug*	*Sep*	*Oct*	*Nov*	*Dec*	*Annual*
El Socorro	10	P	1.8[illegible]	.87	.51	.29	.00	.00	.00	.03	.01	.28	.59	.99	5.42
		T	5[illegible]	58	59	60	62	63	68	68	67	65	62	58	62
El Rosario	12	P	1.0[illegible]	.73	.36	.20	.04	.03	.00	.00	.08	.19	.35	.74	3.72
		T	5[illegible]	59	60	62	64	66	71	73	71	66	62	59	64
Vizcaíno	8	P	.3[illegible]	.54	.08	.02	.00	.00	.11	.04	.70	.15	.23	.91	3.15
		T	5[illegible]	59	60	62	64	65	70	72	70	67	62	59	64
Average		P	.6[illegible]	.64	.22	.11	.02	.02	.06	.02	.39	.17	.29	.83	4.09
		T	58	59	60	61	63	65	70	71	69	66	62	59	63

*Data from Hastings and Humphrey, 1969a.

TABLE 5.5

Mean monthly precipitation and temperature data for 3 gulf coast, Baja California, weather stations within the latitudinal distribution of *Idria**

Station	*Years of Record*	*Precip. (in) Temp. (F)*	*Jan*	*Feb*	*Mar*	*Apr*	*May*	*Jun*	*Jul*	*Aug*	*Sep*	*Oct*	*Nov*	*Dec*	*Annual*
San Luis Gonzaga	1	P	.[illegible]9	.38	.00	.00	.00	.00	.00	.24	.28	.40	.00	.09	2.18
		T	[illegible]9	62	54	69	74	85	89	91	88	80	73	60	75
Bahía de Los Angeles	13	P	.41	.27	.36	.04	.00	.00	.21	.12	.95	.17	.15	.56	2.94
		T	60	62	64	70	76	81	88	88	85	79	69	63	74
El Barril	11	P	.28	.16	.09	.00	.00	.00	.26	.62	1.51	.63	.37	.76	4.68
		T	61	63	65	70	75	82	87	87	85	78	69	63	74
Average		P	.[illegible]9	.27	.05	.01	.00	.00	.16	.33	.91	.40	.17	.47	3.27
		T	60	62	65	70	75	82	88	89	86	75	70	62	74

*Data from Hastings and Humphrey, 1969a.

the interior, they were consistently higher every month of the year, reaching a maximum spread of about ten degrees during the summer months from May through September. These higher coastal temperatures during one or both of the precipitation periods, combined with lower rainfall, appear to be critically limiting for the establishment of *Idria* near the coast.

Mean annual precipitation for the gulf coast stations was 3.26″ as compared with 4.44″ in the interior. However, probably of even greater importance than this difference in total annual precipitation is the difference in rainfall during the winter months from December through March. During this period, which, as has been indicated previously, appears to be the critical time for germination and establishment of the boojum, the coastal stations received on the average only 1.28″ as compared with slightly more than twice this, or 2.74″, in the interior.

Gulf coast of Sonora

The geographic distribution of *Idria* in Sonora, as in Baja California, appears to be determined by climate. Not only do both areas have a bimodal precipitation pattern, they also have very nearly the same mean annual precipitation of between 4.0 and 4.5″ (tables 5.6, 5.1).

The seasonal pattern within *Idria*'s range on the coast of Sonora is similar to that of the peninsular gulf coast at about the same latitude. This seasonal alternation of winter rains, spring drought, summer rains, and fall drought is characteristic of most of the Sonoran Desert. The length of each season, the severity of the periods of drought, and the amount of precipitation that falls during the wet periods may vary from place to place, but the fundamental pattern remains.

The period of record for the Secretaria de Recursos Hidráulicos' stations at Puerto Libertad and Desemboque, the only nearby official weather stations, is too short, seven and four years respectively, to provide very reliable means. The SRH records, however, are supplemented by data obtained in an earlier study by Mallery (1936a,b) and by a three-year record obtained during the present investigation. Mallery's records, obtained during the period 1925 to 1935, gave 4.68″ as the mean annual precipitation at Puerto Libertad and 4.08″ at Punta Cirio, six miles to the south. The rains that fell during the present study at Punta Cirio from December 1967 through November 1970 indicated a mean annual figure of 4.33″.

Although all three records show the bimodal character of the rainfall, only the SRH gages give the amounts on a monthly basis. Those in the current study, as well as those maintained by Mallery, were read at greater than monthly intervals at such times as travel into the area could

TABLE 5.6

Mean monthly precipitation and temperature data for 3 gulf coast, Sonora, weather stations*

Station	Years of Record	Precip. (in) Temp. (F)	Jan	Feb	Mar	Apr	May	Jun	Jul	Aug	Sep	Oct	Nov	Dec	Annual
Puerto Libertád	6	P	.75	.24	.04	.02	.00	.01	.19	.56	.55	.76	.26	1.17	4.55
		T	54	56	58	65	71	74	84	85	82	73	65	56	69
Desemboque	2	P	.26	.30	.24	.00	.00	.07	.68	.63	.06	.31	.51	1.10	4.16
		T	54	55	58	65	71	74	86	85	83	77	65	59	69
Puerto Peñasco	19	P	.29	.22	.15	.04	.00	.01	.17	.38	.57	.64	.24	.69	3.40
		T	52	55	58	64	70	77	85	86	82	73	62	54	68
Average		P	.51	.27	.14	.01	.00	.04	.44	.60	.31	.54	.39	1.14	4.36
		T	54	56	58	65	71	74	85	85	83	75	65	58	69

*Data from Hastings and Humphrey, 1969b.

be arranged. Evaporation from the accumulated precipitation was prevented by a protective cover of motor oil placed in the gages.

Mallery's record, which, because of its greater length, should be the most reliable, shows that roughly 60 percent of the annual rainfall at Punta Cirio falls during the portion of the year that includes the summer months of July, August, and September, the remaining 40 percent falling during the cooler portion that includes the winter months from December through March. The official record at Puerto Libertad is not appreciably different, with 58 and 42 percent respectively for these same seasons. As indicated in table 5.6, however, winter temperatures are markedly lower than those of the summer, thus increasing the effectiveness of the winter rains.

As in Baja California, the coincidence of the availability of ripe boojum seed during the winter rainy season and the high evaporation rate during the summer suggest that germination and establishment rarely, if ever, occur during the summer. The summer rains would seem to function largely in breaking the long spring and foresummer drought and replenishing the dwindling supply of water stored in the small stems of the young boojums. Although this replenishment is not always sufficient to produce a new crop of leaves, it probably plays an essential role in tiding the plants over until the winter rains.

Restriction of the boojums at the Sonora location almost entirely to slopes with a northerly exposure, their occurrence only in a limited area near the gulf where onshore moisture-bearing winds increase the relative humidity, and the smaller stature of the plants than in the Central Desert of the peninsula, suggest a degree of aridity approaching both establishment and growth limits for the species.

Reduction of summer precipitation effectiveness by protracted high summer temperatures may be the ultimate single factor that increases the aridity to a near-lethal level. Although the mean annual temperature statistics show a difference of only two degrees between the Central Desert and the Sonoran coastal study area, the monthly averages reveal that from April through November the Sonoran coast is warmer, particularly during July, August, and September. The Sonora area records a mean temperature of 85, 85, and 83 F respectively for these months as compared with 78, 79 and 76 F in the Central Desert (see tables 5.6, 5.1).

Data are not available on either wind velocities or relative humidity for either region, and any conclusions with reference to these factors must be based on personal but nonquantitative observations. These have been obtained during the many trips that we have made over a period of many years in both Sonora and Baja California. Although subjected to a wide variety of windy conditions, the interior Central Desert does not seem to experience the persistent winds of the Sonoran coastal area. Along the Sonoran coast the winds blow almost constantly, typically onshore in the daytime and offshore at night. The onshore winds carry a sensible moisture load, which increases one's personal discomfort during the heat of the summer. The humidity usually first becomes noticeable some ten to 15 miles from the gulf but increases rapidly within the last two to three miles.

Although the range of mountains in which *Idria* occurs extends inland for a distance of from five to ten miles, the boojum is restricted for most of its approximate north-south 30-mile range to a narrow coastal strip about two miles wide. This is the same coastal area most affected by the onshore moisture-bearing winds, and suggests that without this higher humidity the boojums would not have been able to maintain themselves.

Only a single weather station is to be found along the gulf coast north of Puerto Libertad, consequently few climatic data are available for this area. The one station, Puerto Peñasco, which lies approximately 100 miles NNW of Puerto Libertad, has a recorded mean annual rainfall of 3.4″ (table 5.6). Mean monthly temperatures are almost identical with those at Libertad. Most of the difference in mean annual precipitation derives from a lower winter precipitation at the more northerly station, particularly during December and January. It is probable that this deficiency increases rather consistently with distance north along the coast from Libertad, as there are no physiographic changes or other known factors in this area that might otherwise affect the precipitation.

The marginal conditions under which the boojum manages to survive along the coast south of Libertad, conditions that seem to represent the extreme aridity under which establishment is possible, and the greater aridity north of there, lead to the conclusion that drought is the prime factor preventing its advance to the north. If, as has been proposed, germination and establishment are restricted to the winter months, precipitation during December and January is probably too light to provide the necessary moisture for this all-important phase of the life cycle.

There seems to be no very logical reason for the failure of the boojum to occur further south than it now does along the coast of Sonora. Both temperature and precipitation appear to favor its establishment even more than they do in the Sierra Bacha where it is growing. In the vicinity of Guaymas, for example, the mean annual rainfall is 9.26″, of which 1.5″ falls during the winter (December, January, and February) and 6.39″ during the summer (July, August, and September). There are no coastal weather stations between Desemboque and Guaymas, but records from three others fairly close to the coast and about midway between these two indicate much the same seasonal regimes and mean annual records. Summer temperatures in the stations to the south range about two degrees higher, but it would seem that the considerably higher summer rainfall should more than compensate for this.

There are no apparent differences in either wind velocities or relative humidity that might conceivably prevent the spread of the boojum to the south. Nor do there seem to be any soil or physiographic characteristics that might prevent its southward extension. Perhaps one or more factors that limit it to its present range have been overlooked in this attempt to account for the present limited distribution in Sonora. If, as seems probable, some aspect of climate provides the key, additional kinds of data and a longer period of record may some day provide the answer.

6

General Appearance, Growth Characteristics, and Phenology

Most descriptions of the boojum are based on unbranched individuals seen under average or better-than-average growing conditions. They do not include the many plants at these same locations that differ from the ideal, or those in an unfavorable environment that may differ so markedly as to bear little resemblance to the ideal.

No matter how one describes the boojum, he sooner or later encounters either separate individuals or whole hillsides covered with plants that apparently bear little or no resemblance to his original description. Only the floral structure, the internal anatomy, and certain morphological features serve as identifying characteristics, and these are lost to the casual or untrained observer.

A stem succulent

On the basis of Shreve's classification of Sonoran Desert plants (1951), *Idria* is a "non-succulent woody perennial." It would seem more appropriate to classify the species as a stem-succulent, even though it does have a woody cylinder that gives it the strength to persist for hundreds of years and to reach extreme heights, even though subjected at times to high winds. This cylinder or "skeleton" (figs. 6.1, 6.2) is similar to that of many cacti, the sahuaro *(Carnegiea gigantea)* and the cardón *(Pachycereus pringlei)* as examples. These cacti consist in large part of parenchyma or thin-walled cells of water-storage tissue located both within and without the woody xylem cylinder. The boojum, by contrast, has its parenchymatous water-storage tissues almost entirely in the massive central pith area inside the woody cylinder. It is, however, soft and succulent, and, as in the case of the cacti, has water storage as a prime function (Humphrey, 1935).

The boojum is by many standards one of the most unusual and even bizarre plants not only of the western hemisphere, but of the entire

Fig. 6.1. Skeleton or cylinder of woody vascular tissue of dead boojum. The numbers indicate branch-scar helices and phyllotaxis.

Fig. 6.2. Disintegrating boojum skeleton with representative Central Desert vegetation in the background.

world. For this reason, it is of interest to see how it has appeared to four different individuals: a historian, a biologist, an ecologist, and a philosopher, essayist, and writer of note. These descriptions vary, sometimes because they represent an impression gained after seeing only a few individuals, sometimes because of differences in imagination and ability to convey visual impressions in graphic terms, and sometimes because the objectives of a scientist in describing a plant may differ from those of other writers.

That of the historian Clavijero, first published in 1789 (Clavijero, 1937, pp. 57–58), contains what is assumed to be the first published description of *Idria.*

Much more curious is another tree called *milapa* by the Cochimies, which is found frequently from 29° to 31°. It had not been seen by the missionaries before the year 1751, because they had not gone into the interior of that country. Nor do I believe that it has been known until now by naturalists. It is so large that it grows perpendicularly to a height of seventy feet. Its trunk, thick in proportion, is not woody but soft and succulent like the branches of the *pitajo* and the *cardon.* Its branches are certain little twigs about a foot and a half long, covered with small leaves and protected by a thorn on the end; they do not extend upward or horizontally, as the branches of other trees do, but they hang downward like a beard, from the top to the bottom of the trunk, and the top produces some little bunches of flowers, where no fruit is ever seen. No use is made of this great tree; it is neither dry nor good for firewood, but at the Mission of San Francisco de Borja they burn it because of the lack of fuel.

The description given by Nelson (1922), who was fundamentally a zoologist, is one of the best from a technical point of view:

The cirio *(Idria columnaris)* . . . is a tapering, polelike tree growing from 20 to 50 feet high, with short, slender and thorny branchlets forming a bristling armament along its trunk. This strange tree has tufts of pale yellow flowers rising on long slender stems from the tip of the trunk, which is covered with a smooth greenish-yellow bark. The tapering yellowish trunk and rootletlike branches give the cirio a close resemblance to a gigantic slender parsnip bottom side up.

This is correct as far as it goes but it describes only rather typical plants in favorable habitats; the ideal individual, rather than the many that have deviated from the norm for reasons genetic or other.

As described by Shreve (1951), an ecologist:

Idria ranks without rival as the most bizarre plant of the Sonoran Desert. . . . In fact it is one of the most striking woody plants in the flora of North America. . . . In mature trees the basal diameter of the trunk is 50 to 60 cm., or, exceptionally, as much as 75 cm. In many individuals the trunk tapers gradually from the base; in others it increases in diameter to a height of about 1 to 2 m. and then tapers gradually. The extreme top of the tree, from 6 or 8 m. to the tip, maintains a more uniform diameter of 6 to 12 cm. The trunk is brownish gray and covered by a smooth series of epidermal layers which are heavily permeated with mechanical tissue. The trunk is usually single to the top but is sometimes branched. A wholly distinct type of short, slender branch is also borne on the lower part of the trunk. This type has a horizontal position, is repeatedly branched, and bears leaves but never flowers. The branches of the latter type arise from the trunk at regularly spaced intervals on great spirals, as if conforming to a very precise form of phyllotaxy.

And as Joseph Wood Krutch (1961), an essayist and writer, saw it:

What, then, is this astonishing tree like? The right answer is "like nothing else on earth," though the commonest description is "like an upsidedown carrot, improbably provided with slender, spiny, and usually leafless branches which seem to be stuck helter-skelter into the tapering, carroty body." . . . But fully grown specimens can reach a height of forty or fifty feet, tapering to a point from a base only a foot or eighteen inches in diameter — which is far too slender for a respectable carrot. Moreover, they often branch in an absent-minded manner toward the upper end, and sometimes, as though embarrassed by their inordinate length, curve downward until the tip touches the earth and thus becomes what is perhaps the only tree which makes a twenty-foot-high arch like a gateway into a wizard's garden.

Variations from the norm

Careful analysis of those individuals on the better interior sites might show that the general shape and aspect of the boojum differ from the norm no more than do those of most other plants. Perhaps they only seem to because the plant's basic simplicity makes any lapse from accepted standards more noticeable. Whether this is so or not, certain it is that even on the best sites the plants are highly individualistic, and a rather large percentage do not fit the standard descriptions. Many, for example, are straight, tall, and unbranched (fig. 6.3), while others grow as twins, triplets, or may have up to at least ten separate stems arising from ground level (fig. 6.4); still others branch only above ground, sometimes in an apparently haphazard manner (fig. 6.5), sometimes as a result of breakage of the original stem (fig. 6.6), and occasionally in a definite pattern of dichotomy (fig. 6.7).

Despite the usual descriptions of *Idria* as a slender, polelike tree and the name "cirio" implying a slender candlelike appearance, the plant is a potential contortionist throughout its range and in addition may be anything but polelike where it is exposed to chilling winds, high humidity, and frequent fogs along the Pacific coast. There the plants might be more correctly described as follows:

Fig. 6.3. *Idria* as an unbranched candlelike tree. From this form it derives the name "cirio."

Fig. 6.4. Unusual boojum with ten main trunks all originating at or near ground level. All of the trunks cannot be distinguished in this picture.

Fig. 6.5. The boojum as it sometimes branches in an apparently haphazard or absent-minded manner. Note the individuals in the background branching in a stricter, more typical fashion.

Fig. 6.6. Branching stimulated by breaking of the original stem. Remains of original woody vascular tissue still persist in the crotch.

Fig. 6.7. Example of dichotomous branching in a 60-foot-tall boojum. *Lophocereus schottii* in the near foreground.

Fig. 6.8. Pacific coastal boojum in full leaf and variously contorted.

Fig. 6.9. Pacific coastal boojum typically contorted and short in stature. Other misshapen individuals are visible in the distance.

A woody plant, sometimes treelike, but usually no more than ten to 12 or at times only two to three feet tall with thorny, twiglike, lateral branches along a sometimes simple or sparingly branched, but often variously branched and contorted, main stem (figs. 6.8–6.11). The smooth bark is occasionally whitish, but is usually black, gray, or green. In the more exposed situations close to the Pacific coast the main stem is short, gnarled, and stubby (fig. 6.12), or the entire plant may be clothed with lichens (fig. 6.13).

Phyllotaxis

The description by Shreve (1951) contains the interesting comment: "The branches . . . arise from the trunk at regularly spaced intervals on great spirals, as if conforming to a very precise form of phyllotaxy."* This observation focused our attention on this aspect of the boo-

*Phyllotaxy: the arrangement of leaves or floral parts on their axis.

Fig. 6.10. Many-branched Pacific coastal boojum showing tendency of drooping branches to grow always upward.

Fig. 6.11. Abnormally distorted Pacific coastal boojum. Here the heavy stems rest on the ground but have not rooted. The ends of the stems are typically growing upward against gravity.

Fig. 6.12. Eighteen-inch-high, mature and apparently very old boojum in an exposed situation about one-fourth mile from the Pacific.

Fig. 6.13. Not a fir tree, but a leafless, lichen-covered boojum close to the Pacific coast. The plant is thriving despite apparent handicaps of little soil, a harsh climate, and a smothering epiphyte.

jum and ultimately resulted in our making many observations and branch-gap counts. As a result we have concluded that the plant does indeed possess distinct phyllotaxic characteristics, although this phyllotaxis or arrangement of branches is not exactly precise.

The buds, and from these the branches, are arranged in distinct spirals, or helices, which on a given plant can be followed in both clockwise and counter-clockwise directions to form a double helix (figs. 6.1, 6.14). These spirals are readily visible on the living plants, or even more easily on the occasional dead skeletons where most of the tissues except the woody cylinder of xylem have disintegrated and largely fallen away (fig. 6.1).

It is not possible to distinguish definite spirals or helices on all plants because of the interposition of anomalous branches that confuse the normal helical series. This is particularly likely to characterize abnormally large individuals which, apparently as a result of greater age, have had a greater opportunity to form additional lateral meristematic tissue that ultimately develops as supernumerary branches.

The boojum is extremely long-lived, and although it cannot be said that dead individuals occur rarely, they at least are not a common feature of the landscape. Those that do die fall over or disintegrate within a few years, so that only occasional standing skeletons are encountered. Of these few, only a small percentage have branch-scar spirals that are not confused by anomalous gaps. Consequently, it has not been possible to obtain data from a sufficient number of dead trees to provide material for any sort of statistical analysis. Observations were made on 13 specimens, however, that at least suggest certain phyllotaxic characteristics for the species (table 6.1).

Note that 11 of the 13 boojums had either seven or eight spirals interposed before any given spiral was again visible on the same side of the trunk. The two records of 13 interposed helices indicate that there may be considerable deviation from the more typical seven or eight pattern.

Interpreting the counts made on plants 6 to 13 in terms of the Fibonacci fractional series (see Featherly, 1965, for an explanation) we thus have four Fibonacci series of 8/20, and one each of 8/17, 7/17, 13/22, and 13/25. Because of the vertical distance involved in making a complete cycle and the difficulty in determining when a branch scar is anatomically, and thus truly, above the beginning scar, exact interpretation or reading of the series is difficult. Thus experimental error in each of the numerators in these series could account for a reasonable variation one unit larger or smaller than the recorded count. Despite this, however, there is believed to be no possibility of errors in counting that could

Fig. 6.14. Clockwise and counter-clockwise helices marked on *Idria* trunk.

TABLE 6.1

Boojum phyllotaxis

Boojum No.	*No. of interposed helices*	*No. of branch gaps per helix*
1	8	Not counted
2	8	" "
3	7	" "
4	7	" "
5	7	" "
6	8	20
7	8	17
8	7	17
9	8	20
10	8	20
11	8	20
12	13	22
13	13	25

account for a variation in the denominator ranging from 17 to 25. Therefore, while the most common Fibonacci series may be 8/20 or even 7/20 or 8/21, the counts do definitely indicate a variable, rather than a constant, series.

Stem types

Idria has two kinds of stems, one greatly thickened and succulent (figs. 6.15, 6.16), the other essentially nonsucculent (figs. 6.16, 6.17). As an aid to clarity, these will be referred to as stems and branches respectively. Thus, by definition, the stems are the succulent main trunk or trunks including any similar, succulent branching trunks; the branches are the relatively short, essentially nonsucculent side branches with which the main trunks are usually covered. Very occasionally a side branch may turn up at the end and develop succulence and its own side branches. In this case the modified branch will be referred to as a stem.

Stem growth

Terminal growth of the stems or main trunks apparently occurs only during the winter-spring period, never during the summer or at any other season of the year (see table 6.3, page 84). The amount of growth, as indicated by increase in stem length, may be considerable during years with unusually effective winter rains. This may contrast with little or no growth during years of extreme drought. Because of the erratic precipitation in the Central Desert and on the coast of Sonora, it is highly probable that several periods of successive years have often occurred during the lifetime of most mature boojums during which there has been no growth.

Even during the short interval of this investigation we have recorded three years when no growth was recorded at some locations and two when the rate could be considered as average to exceptional. As examples of these extremes, the winter of 1967–68 was exceptionally wet in much or perhaps all of the Central Desert, while the following winter was unusually dry. In the Sonoran area the winter of 1969–70 had good rains but almost none a year later.

At one Central Desert location that we came to know as Gold Mine Camp, current terminal growth was measured March 19, 1968 on 23 plants that ranged in height from seven inches to eight feet. Twenty of these were actively growing, and had new terminal growth that ranged from less than one up to seven inches and averaged 2.27 inches (fig. 6.16). Five plants had new growth of four inches or more.

These measurements may represent very nearly an optimum rate for the plants in their native habitat. In contrast, no growth was recorded at this location the following spring. Quoting from my notes of June 12,

Fig. 6.15. Young boojum with branches removed. Plant Is 5 ft. 9 in. tall.

Fig. 6.16. Actively growing main stem and side branches of boojum. Thick-petioled terminal primary leaves indicate current year's growth.

Fig. 6.17. Boojum side branches, showing primary leaf blades at tip of developing spines and fascicles of secondary leaves in axils of primary leaves and spines.

1969: "After searching thoroughly for about half an hour we were unable to find any *Idria*s with new terminal growth. Some had a few young branches at the top, but there seems to have been no terminal growth on any of the plants this last spring. We looked especially at the young plants in the age class that grows most rapidly — those from about three to ten feet tall. Even on these there was no new growth. The lack of growth is in marked contrast to our observations last year in this same area."

In the Sonoran coastal area the winter of 1969–70 was a "good" one as indicated by such phenological characteristics as leaf formation, flowering, and stem elongation on many of the perennial woody species, as well as by rainfall records and soil moisture penetration. My field notes under the date of Feb. 13, 1970, taken at a disjunct colony of about 30 boojums about a quarter-mile north of the main population, read: *"Punta Cirio, Sonora, Idria Colony*. All *Idria*s growing rapidly. Excellent terminal growth. One plant with 6 inches new growth."

In contrast with 1970, none of the plants in this colony had produced any current terminal growth when they were observed on March 14, 1971 and on June 9, 1972. That the plants were being subjected to a period of severe winter drought was indicated by the precipitation record from a rain gage located a half-mile distant. The March 1971 reading showed only .24 inches precipitation since it had last been read on December 1, 1970, or less than a quarter of an inch in more than three months during the "winter rainy period." The following year even less was recorded: .18 inches from December 13, 1971 to June 9, 1972.

From these and many other observations made during the course of the study, it is obvious that despite the water-storage capability of the boojum, the amount of terminal stem growth on different plants, even within a restricted area, or in any given year, is extremely variable. Also, as in the case of the February 13 observation at Punta Cirio, that growth may be considerable at times even prior to what might usually be thought of as the spring growing season. These various measurements do not indicate the maximum possible stem growth that may occur in any given year. They indicate only that stem growth varies widely within certain limits and may range from none to at least as much as seven inches.

Growth over a three-year period on boojums transplanted and growing near Tucson, Arizona, tend to corroborate the observations made in Baja California and Sonora relative to season of stem growth. Despite the fact that plants ranging in height from one inch to three feet have been kept watered throughout this period, measurable terminal growth has been restricted to the late winter and early spring months on all plants except seedlings up to one year old.

Idria the contortionist

"Cirio" suggests something tall, straight, and gradually tapering, "boojum" something weird, unpredictable, and even frightening, a grotesque kind of monstrosity, growing in far-off dangerous lands (Carroll, 1966). If *Idria* is a cirio, it is just as surely a boojum. It is probable that all little boojums begin life with chromosomal cirio instructions. Sooner or later, however, these directives are forgotten and the boojum takes over.

Few plants in the desert can properly be described as contorted, but this is the word that most often comes to mind when one sees the grotesque forms assumed by many *Idria*s. One wonders whether they are really more contorted than other plants, or whether the simple nature of their main stem structure, poorly hidden at best by the spare side branches, merely makes apparent a condition typical of most other woody species. That which we see is not necessarily that which is. Nonetheless, what we see leaves an impression, and the impression here is that the boojum as a contortionist has no equal in the Sonoran Desert.

Despite the knowledge that it is not so, after long exposure to the boojum and the harsh environment from which it cannot escape, one cannot avoid the empathetic feeling that here is a plant in agony, writhing under a torture it must endure, even for centuries (fig. 6.18).

The simplest deviation from the pure cirio form is a relaxed drooping of the stem, as though the plant just lacked the strength to remain upright. Simple as this explanation is, it probably explains not only this least complicated variation from the ideal, but probably most of the more complex forms as well.

*Idria*s are structurally strong because of the peripheral cylinder of woody tissue. They can withstand wind velocities far in excess of those that seemingly should snap off the main stem. In fact, they intercept little wind and bend only slightly even under high velocities. Because of the large amounts of thin-walled water-storage tissues in the central pith, however, they are heavy, and, unless growing in a vertical position, this weight puts a continuing and bending strain on the relatively thin woody cylinder. As a consequence, the stem not infrequently bends and cannot right itself. At the same time the tip continues to grow and, as proper plants should, to grow upward, not downward (figs. 6.10, 6.11). This new growth merely adds to the weight already there, and the stem continues to droop. The tip, or tips in the multibranched plants, may reach the ground where they finally rest, but even here the growing ends always point upward.

These simultaneously exerted forces of weight and growth, continuously operating through the years, leave their impress on the plant

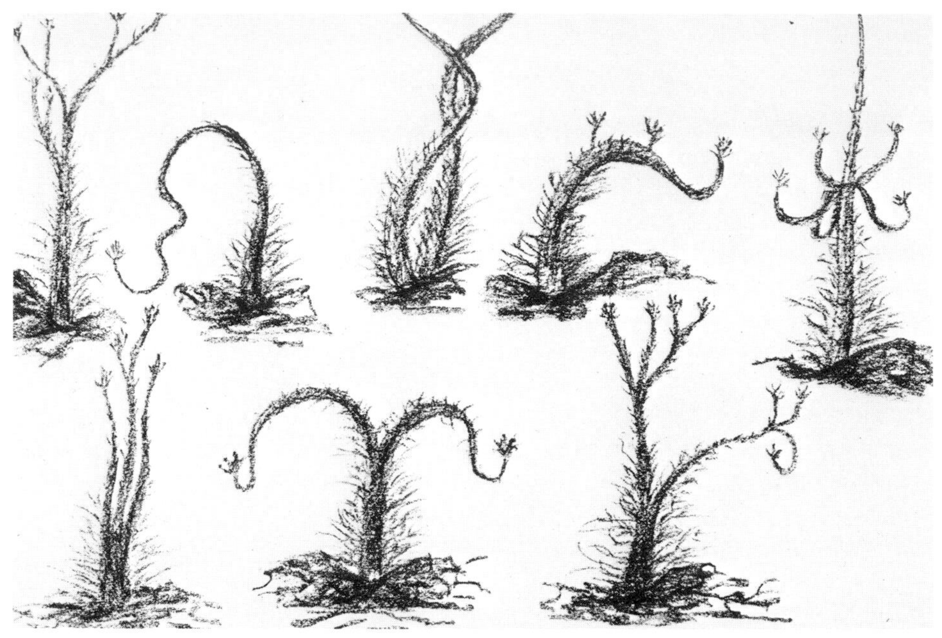

Fig. 6.18. *Idria* the contortionist — variations on a theme.
Drawings by Roberta Humphrey.

and their impression on the eye as contortion in varying degrees and a variety of shapes.

Branch growth

The side branches, in marked contrast with the main stems, are relatively slender and, as has been indicated, are essentially nonsucculent. They serve almost entirely to produce and support the leaves or, occasionally, flowers. When young, these branches appear always to bear spines that develop as a part of the petiole of the primary leaf (figs. 6.16, 6.17). When these leaves are shed an extension of the cortical tissue that served initially as the apparent lower or abaxial side of the petiole remains to form a slender, sharp-pointed spine (Humphrey, 1931, 1935).

The branches may persist for many years with little or no change except gradual elongation and some proliferation of secondary branches. In time, many of them develop some secondary thickening and, through gradual weathering of the spines, become spineless (figs. 6.19, 6.20). In this state they appear distinctly different from the usual slender, spiny form. Although the two aspects have been described as distinct kinds of branches, it is probable that the spineless form is merely a developmental stage of an initially spiny branch.

We have come to refer to the spineless form as a short-shoot spur

Fig. 6.19. Dwarf branches of boojum with disintegrating spines.

Fig. 6.20. Boojum with dwarf branches presumably older than in fig. 6.19, with spines entirely weathered away.

or dwarf branch. And, even though apparently only a developmental expression, they are distinctly different from the spiny branches and merit additional description.

Each fascicle of leaves that is borne in the axil of the primary leaf and its spine represents a potential branch. This potential may be realized in varying degrees, ranging from zero to a fraction of a millimeter or more in length for each crop of leaves. Where there is a slight increment, and this typically occurs once or sometimes twice a year, a dwarf branch gradually develops. When these are small they are usually subtended by the original spine, although this is often vestigial. Ultimately, it drops off or weathers away.

As the dwarf branches gradually elongate, they and the main branch to which they are attached gradually increase in diameter. Main branches 5 mm or less in diameter usually still have at least vestiges of spines remaining; others, even though no larger, may bear no trace of spines. Except where these branches end in one or more dwarf branches they are no longer elongating and consequently no longer producing primary leaves with their attendant spines.

As the dwarf branches grow, the diameter of the branches that bear them slowly increases. There is no specific limit to this thickening, but they often reach a characteristic diameter of about 2 cm. Their age when this size, or even ultimately, is a moot question, since they do not form identifiable growth rings.

The dwarf branches may, in turn, occasionally branch. More typically, though, they continue to develop as single stems, with leaves forming only at the tip as seen in fig. 6.21. As a fascicle of leaves is formed and shed, which usually happens either once or twice a year, the petiole dehisces obliquely. These leaf scars gradually shrivel and in time remain as minor wrinkles, each extending part way around the stub branch. A count of these in a vertical line from the base of the branch to its tip is believed to indicate the number of crops of leaves a given branch has borne. Individual branches vary widely in the discernibility of these wrinkles or scars. Scar counts of 83, 86, 89, and 101 were recorded on four stub branches that ranged in length from 35 to 45 mm. Both the branch lengths and the number of scars seemed to be representative of these kinds of data on other boojums in the area. Obviously, in no sense of the word could these branches be considered as a representative sample. They may, however, be accepted as an indication of the extremely slow growth rate of the dwarf branches. If, as may be, each scar lying directly above the one below indicates either a half or full year's growth, these branches, despite their short length, have taken from about 40 to 100 years to grow. Even assuming that two crops of leaves were developed 50 percent of the time, an age of 50 to 75 years can be postulated. And during this period the branches assumed a total maximum length of only 45 mm or about 1¾ inches.

The dwarf branches are characteristically short. Seventy-three of them were measured on three branches collected at random from trees in the Sonoran colony. These 73 branches ranged in length from 13 to 50 mm and averaged 37 mm. Of these, slightly more than half, or 55 percent, fell in the 30 to 40 mm length class; only one measured less than 20 mm and only one was recorded at the maximum length of 50 mm.

The basal branches have an occasional tendency to be spiny, while those on the upper several feet of the stem are spineless and often very

Fig. 6.21. Fascicles of secondary leaves on the tips of dwarf branches. Dark spots on the leaves are aphids.

short. This shortness may give the upper several feet of the stem the appearance of having no branches, particularly when the plants are in full leaf and the short branches tend to be obscured (fig. 6.22). Whether spiny or not, the basal branches are usually longer than those higher up, probably in some instances because they are older and have had greater opportunity to elongate.

The usual spiny branches may be simple, with no side branches of their own, or they may proliferate rather extensively. Damage to the terminal bud often induces this proliferation. Although the dwarf branches occasionally develop similar dwarf side branches, this is not always the case. In some instances typical spiny branches may originate from latent meristematic tissue of a branch that bears principally or exclusively dwarf branches.

New branches soon develop on the main stem when the original ones have been removed or otherwise damaged (fig. 6.23). Even removal of all the side branches has no apparent deleterious effect on the plant except possibly to expose it for a few months to potential damage from foraging animals. Even such damage, however, is minimal, as the boojum seems to be unpalatable to most foraging and leaf-eating animals, whether they are larger herbivores, rodents, or insects.

The side branches may grow during any season. Usually, however, they develop most rapidly when the precipitation-evaporation ratio is most favorable and has been so for a considerable period (see table 6.3, page 84). These conditions usually prevail during the late winter and

Fig. 6.22. Boojum with short branches on upper part of stem and longer ones below.

Fig. 6.23. Young boojum on which branches were removed as in fig. 6.15 two years prior to the date of this photo. Note extensive branch regeneration.

early spring months of February, March, and April, but may recur during July, August, and September.

Current growth on both the main stems and side branches is readily recognized by leaf and spine development (fig. 6.16). The primary leaves remain attached until drought ensues, usually for a period of only four to six months. Terminal growth ends a short time before the leaves drop. As primary leaves are produced only on new growth, only those portions of the main stem or side branches with primary leaves can have developed during the current growth period, thus making it easy to determine the most recent amount of increment.

Rate of branch growth

The maximum growth recorded for a single season on individual branches was noted in Baja California on plants growing between Laguna Chapala and Punta Prieta (Gold Mine Camp) on March 20, 1968. On this occasion the new growth on both stems and branches was measured on 23 plants. Growth increment was highly variable, but the three plants that showed the maximum current branch development had individual branches on which the current increments were recorded as 25, 27, and 35 inches. In all instances, these figures represented new growth on branches that were still actively elongating and their final length by the onset of the summer drought is unknown.

Leaves and spines

Idria's leaves and spines have characteristics that are distinctive of the family, if not the genus. The present study has disclosed nothing new or unusual in the kinds of leaves the plant bears, except in certain aspects of their development and shedding.

It has long been known, for example, that *Idria,* like all members of the family, has two kinds of leaves, commonly referred to as primary and secondary (Engelmann, 1883; Poisson, 1895; Van Tieghem, 1899; Robinson, 1904; Reiche, 1922; Humphrey, 1931, 1935). The primary leaves are borne singly and only on the growing ends of the main stems or side branches. As the apical meristem continues to grow and the stems and branches elongate, the primary leaves and developing spines are left behind on the elongating stem as lateral leaves and spines.

Spines are formed on the newly developing stems and side branches as an apparent integral part of the primary leaves. These are formed as what appears to be the lower or abaxial portion of the petiole or leaf stem. The spine is not technically a part of the petiole but is, instead, an extension of the stem cortex or bark that is attached to the petiole for its entire length. When the leaf is shed the petiole separates from the cortical extension, leaving a sharp-pointed spine. So far as known there is no other member of the plant kingdom that forms spines in this fashion.

The secondary leaves are borne as fascicles or clusters in the axils of these spines. This positioning is the same, whether the leaves are borne on the main stem or the branches. After the primary leaves have been shed, new ones never develop at the same position or on the same wood. This is in contrast to the secondary leaves, new fascicles of which continue to develop year after year from the same bud tissues at the identical axillary location. Thus, each fascicle is in reality a greatly foreshortened branch which, although it may never become long enough to resemble a branch, does, nonetheless, contain this potential. As pointed out earlier, these fascicular dwarf branches may very gradually elongate as successive clumps of leaves form on their ends and are shed.

Idria, like the other members of the family, may produce more than one crop of leaves per year. Leaf growth is apparently controlled largely by soil moisture and water balance and may occur at any time of the year. The proper conditions usually prevail soon after the onset of the winter rains, but may also occur during the summer rainy season during years of exceptionally favorable summer storms (see table 6.3, page 84).

Shreve (1951, p. 38) appears never to have seen *Idria* with leaves in the summer and concluded that it bore leaves only during the winter. In fact, although it may be leafless during the long spring-summer-fall period, it may develop a full crop of leaves during the summer. We first observed this in 1967 at Punta Cirio in Sonora. On arrival there on August 16 the boojums were all leafless, the soil was dry, and the ocotillo (*Fouquieria splendens*) and other plants showed no sign of recent rains. That night a light rain fell that moistened the sandy soil to a depth of 1.5 inches. The following day the rains started again at 4 a.m. and fell heavily until 6 a.m., then continued less heavily until 10 a.m. On a sandy soil area with little runoff the moisture at the end of this time had penetrated to a depth of 12 inches.

By the afternoon of the 18th leaves were beginning to show on the ocotillo, and by the 21st were almost fully developed on most plants of this species. By noon of the 22nd, when a previous commitment required that we leave the area, all the ocotillos were in full leaf, but there was no sign of any leaf development yet on the boojum. However, when we returned 16 days later on September 8 we found them all in full leaf. The soil was moist to a depth of 20 inches at the same location where a moisture depth of 12 inches had been recorded 22 days earlier.

Rains the same summer were apparently good in much of the Central Desert of Baja California. The boojum was in full leaf from

September 28 to October 30 at least as far south as Laguna Chapala, which was our turn-around point for that trip.

Additional research may reveal exceptions, but the present study has indicated that the boojum typically sheds its leaves once during the year in the spring period from about mid-March to mid-May. The exact time of shedding, whether early or late during this two-month interval, is determined by the effect of climatic conditions on soil moisture. As the soil moisture content is reduced, the leaves begin to turn yellow and finally to drop. Those of the elephant tree *(Pachycormus discolor)* behave rather similarly, with the result that portions of the desert where these two species are intermixed and abundant, as they often are, develop a golden-yellow aspect. Thus, one has the feeling that he is witnessing a paradox of nature and that autumn has arrived in the spring.

Although no plants that produce leaves in the summer have been observed to shed these leaves during the ensuing fall drought, this is probably because the period of study has been too short. This has been verified by observations on plants grown at Tucson under controlled conditions. Potted plants, for example, that have not been watered quickly shed their leaves at any time of the year. Once the leaves have been shed, the plants are slow in growing new ones. Much additional study is needed to determine the factors that determine leaf development. Perhaps it is largly a matter of time required to permit new leaf primordia to develop, or it may be that, regardless of this development, air and soil temperatures and moisture levels are the final triggering mechanisms.

In summary, certain generalizations may be drawn with regard to leaf behavior. The leaves typically develop during the cool months of November and December, but a second crop may form during the hot months of summer if rains have been exceptionally favorable. They typically turn yellow and are shed as soil moisture drops and temperatures rise during April and May. Except when summer leaves develop, the plants are normally leafless from the latter part of April and May through October or November.

Flowering and seed production

The flowers are usually borne in panicles arising near the tips of the main stems (fig. 6.24) or on specialized panicles that develop at or near the tip of stalks that grow from or near the ends of some of the upper side branches. Abnormally, this latter type of stalk may occur occasionally on these branches for a considerable distance down the trunk.

The fruiting stalks begin growth by about the onset of the spring drought during April and continue growing through June (see table 6.3,

Fig. 6.24. Typical boojum flowers showing usual point of origin at tip of main stem.

page 84). Most of the flowers open during July, August, and September, although the full flowering season is even more protracted than this (fig. 6.25). A few plants with open flowers may sometimes be found as late as the first week in November. These, however, are definitely late bloomers and are atypical.

The flowers are highly aromatic, perfuming the air with a delicate fragrance for many days during the peak of their blossoming period. This attracts a variety of insects ranging from moths and butterflies through flies to a variety of bees and wasps (Humphrey and Werner, 1969). Even beetles and bugs (hemiptera) and an occasional hummingbird are attracted to them, presumably by the nectar or pollen, but perhaps sometimes by insects on which they prey (see Chapter 9 and Appendix B for additional details).

Seed ripening continues over about a two-month period during October and November, usually reaching a peak in most places about the first week in November (fig. 6.26; table 6.3, page 84). Although there may be local differences in the degree of ripeness from one location to another, we have observed no consistency in this regard. Seeds at the northern limits of distribution do not seem to ripen consistently earlier or later than those in the southern areas. Similarly, those in the warm interior seem to ripen at about the same time as those in the much cooler Pacific coastal areas.

The majority of plants of flowering age blossomed profusely and set an abundant crop of seed during each of the four years when flowering and seeding were studied. Despite this, it has been noted that both blossoming and seed set are affected to some extent by drought, particularly in plants that are in their first few years of flowering. Most individuals, however, like those of *Foquieria splendens* and *F. diguetii*, blossomed and set viable seed abundantly with little respect to precipitation during the previous winter and spring. Even when there had been little or no new terminal stem growth, an abundant seed crop was typically produced.

Although the wind-disseminated seeds may be carried some distance from the parent plant, the "wing" area is small with reference to the seed proper and most of them settle to the ground near the parent

Fig. 6.25. *Idria* in bloom.

Fig. 6.26. Seed-bearing panicles of *Idria* showing typical mature seed capsules.

tree. Once ripening has been initiated, the seeds mature rapidly and literally fall in showers when a few quiet days are followed by a day of gusty winds.

Height at flowering

Height at first flowering of the plants seems to be related to the characteristics of the site. Those individuals on the poorer sites tend to be shorter when they first bloom than those on the better sites. Size as related to initiation of flowering would appear to be a function of age, since plants on the better sites grow more rapidly than those where conditions are less favorable. Thus an individual on a relatively arid site with shallow, fine-texture soil may first produce blossoms when five feet tall, whereas one on a deep, medium-texture soil where aridity is less may not bloom until it reaches a height of eight to ten feet.

The Pacific coastal boojums, which never attain the heights of either the interior Central Desert or Sonoran populations, are probably slow growing. In any event, they tend to initiate blooming when comparatively small (table 6.2). In obtaining the data in this table, the height of all

TABLE 6.2
Plant height at initial flowering as related to site

Quadrat	*Site*	*No. of plants measured*	*Ave. ht. plants with flowers (ft)*	*Min. ht. at flowering (ft)*
A	Coastal	19	6.38	2.9
B	"	5	6.34	3.2
C	"	13	5.25	2.1
D	Interior	6	21.7	7.9

boojums in each of three 50 x 100-foot quadrats near the Pacific coast were measured and noted in relation to blooming. Similar data were obtained on a single site 20 miles inland.

It will be noted that there is an obvious marked difference between coastal and interior boojums, both with regard to the average height of the flowering plants and the minimum height at which flowering is recorded. These differences are sufficiently great, and the coastal and interior plants differ sufficiently in general appearance, to suggest distinct populations. This is a possibility, one that may be verified or rejected on the basis of electrophoretic-gel analyses currently under way.

This aspect of the overall investigation is based on a polyacrylamide-gel electrophoretic analysis of amylase and esterase isozymes in the seeds and seedlings of 21 isolated populations. Preliminary results indicate that these populations are highly polymorphic for these isozymes. Although the isozymic patterns show apparent relationships, the populations appear to have been reproductively isolated for a sufficiently long period that genetic relationships between geographically closely associated populations have been largely obscured by genetic drift (Hall, 1972).

The boojum — the tallest tree of the Sonoran Desert?*

The boojum is, with little doubt, the tallest plant in that part of the Sonoran Desert that lies in Baja California, or perhaps in the entire Sonoran Desert.

Foresters have long been inclined to look for the tallest tree of a given species to obtain its vital statistics and to give it due publicity. Outstanding heights have been recorded for some species as, for example, ponderosa pine, Douglasfir, redwood, and eucalyptus. To most foresters, the boojum and cereus-type cacti may not be trees; to many other botanists, on the other hand, they are, and have every right to stand up

* Reprinted with minor changes by permission from *Cactus and Succulent Journal.*

and be counted (or measured) along with other giants of the forests in which they live.

In any event, and for whatever reason, in our study of *Idria* we have been on the lookout for unusually tall individuals and have measured many. In addition, we have attempted to obtain representative height and diameter measurements on typical stands in various parts of the species' range.

Although many travelers in the land of the boojum have been impressed by their height, few have stopped to measure them and fewer still to publish their findings. Forrest Shreve, during his many years of research in the Sonoran Desert, took the time to do both. For example (1951, p. 109):

"*Idria* and *Pachycereus* often attain a height of 14 m., and several exceptional examples have been measured which were over 20 m. . . . The heaviest stands of *Idria* were found in high bajadas near Punta Prieta, on deep, stony volcanic clay." Shreve also notes (p. 106) that in the granitic or gneiss hills of the northern Vizcaíno Region many of the plants are large and "many of them have reached the maximum size of their kind." And (p. 28), "A height of 11 m. is sometimes reached by *Carnegiea* and 16 to 18 m. by *Pachycereus* and *Idria.*" Comparing maximum heights reached by *Idria* in Sonora and Baja California (p. 92) he notes that the tallest individuals in Sonora are 12 to 14 m. high, as compared with the highest known individuals, 22 m. (22 m. = 72 ft 2 in). In no instance does he indicate how these heights were determined.

Nelson (1922, p. 106) described *Idria* as "a tapering, pole-like tree growing from 20 to over 50 feet." Nelson's figures are probably estimates rather than exact measurements. Henrickson (1969) reports that they reach a maximum height of 16 m. (52 ft 6 in).

During the course of the present study, the tallest individuals have been found at two locations with highly permeable soils largely derived from granite. One of these was in a scenic area between Agua Dulce and La Virgen (ca. lat. 29° 50′ N; long. 114° 50′ W Gerhard and Gulick 1967, Map No. 5) studded with picturesque monolithlike granite boulders. The other, about 16 miles from Bahía de Los Angeles by car or by foot, or roughly five airline miles, lies on the west side of the Sierra de Los Angeles (ca. lat. 28° 55′ N; long. 114° 20′ W).

The La Virgen site is a gently rolling to level upland at about 2,000 feet elevation, essentially midway between the gulf and the Pacific Ocean. Mean annual precipitation is about four inches (Hastings and Humphrey, 1969). The Sierra de Los Angeles site, although only about five miles from the gulf, lies at an elevation of 1,500 feet. No detailed climatic data are available, but the mean annual precipitation is estimated at between three and four inches. The terrain is essentially a gently north-sloping bajada intersected by numerous variable-size drainages.

The tallest boojums in the La Virgen area are considerably taller than the average of those in either Baja California or Sonora. The tallest individual that we have seen here, as measured by a Suunto clinometer, measured 72 feet, 6 inches. A second, growing nearby, reached a height of 70 feet. Several others in the general vicinity ranged between 60 and 70 feet.

As was true of the majority of specimens in the La Virgen area, the two tallest were sparingly forked, these few branches being closely appressed to the main stem. The nonsucculent side branches from these stems, like those of most of the cirios in the area, were deeply clothed with leaves that had developed following heavy rains about a month earlier.

The tallest boojum found to date, and presumably thus far recorded, was located at the Sierra de Los Angeles site. Four clinometer measurements taken from as many directions from the plant, gave an average height of 76 feet, 6 inches (fig. 6.27). Maximum basal diameter, which was consistent from one to three feet above ground, was recorded with a K&E diameter tape at 25 feet, 2 inches. Although many other boojums in the vicinity exceeded 60 feet in height, all were at least five feet shorter than the tallest.

The maximum heights that may be reached by individual boojums vary from one location to another. Instances of characteristic height differences were reported earlier (Humphrey & Humphrey, 1969). In this earlier study, four populations were evaluated, three in Baja California and one on the mainland of Sonora. The Baja California populations were classified as Baja Pacifico (Pacific coast), Baja Interior (central interior), and Las Arrastras (a semi-isolated stand near the northeast range of the boojum). The Sonoran population was designated Sierra Bacha.

The analysis was intended as suggestive rather than definitive, but did indicate that distinct mean-maximum height differences do exist from one location to another. These ranged from an average maximum of 55 feet, 2 inches at Baja Interior to 34 feet at Sierra Bacha, 15 feet, 2 inches at Las Arrastras, and 10 feet, 11 inches at Baja Pacifico. As these figures were obtained from measurement of representative numbers of the tallest individuals at the various locations, they are not exactly repeatable. They do, however, indicate definite general maximum height differences that characterize the boojum at these sites.

Fig. 6.27. The tallest cirio, 76 ft. 6 in.

Discussion

The differences in maximum attainable heights are probably most often the result of differences in climate and soil, although preliminary electrophoretic analyses suggest that, in some instances at least, genetic differences may also be involved.

Although a mean annual precipitation of three to four inches might seem offhand to be too little to produce a luxuriant desert vegetation, this is not the case. The soils are deep, highly permeable, and gently sloping, providing ideal conditions for infiltration and water storage. As a consequence, runoff occurs at infrequent intervals and usually in quantity only after the infrequent torrential *chubascos* or hurricanes. Not only the giant boojums, but the size of the other dominants as well, point to a highly efficient use of the limited precipitation.

An added climatic feature conducive to maximum height growth is air movement or wind. The boojum has developed along lines of water storage rather than strength, yet because of its internal structure, slender trunk, and short branches has surprising ability to resist wind breakage. Despite this, however, one does see many individuals whose tops have been snapped off by the wind. This might be expected in view of its height and probable age. (A study under way at the University of Arizona by J. R. Hastings and R. M. Turner indicates a probable age of 700 to 800 years!) The Sierra de Los Angeles site is somewhat protected from high winds by its proximity to the mountains that provide shelter on three sides. The high-velocity winds appear to be carried up and over the mountains, thus creating a kind of pocket below in which the boojums are partly protected.

The La Virgen site is more exposed, but the large granitic monoliths that characterize the area provide a barrier to excessive wind movement near the ground, thus probably reducing stem breakage and facilitating growth to exceptional heights. In addition, there is little doubt that the soil and moisture conditions at both these sites are highly favorable and may be capable of producing taller plants than some other equally protected areas.

In the absence of any exact wind velocity data, I am admittedly speculating in regard to the effect of wind protection in both these instances in an attempt to explain the ability of the boojums to live at these locations for hundreds of years and attain the heights they do without breaking. More detailed later climatic data may indicate otherwise; for the present, however, this conjecture seems plausible.

TABLE 6.3

Idria Columnaris Phenological* Highlights

Month	*Stems & Branches*	*Leaves*	*Flowers*	*Seeds*
Jan	Dormant	Summer Crop (if any) Plus Full Crop of Current Winter	None	None
Feb	Largely Dormant But Dormancy Breaking	In Full Leaf	None	None
Mar	Active Growth	Yellowing and Starting to Fall	None	None
Apr	Somewhat Active But Tapering Off	Yellowing and Falling	Floral Branches Beginning to Elongate	None
May	Stems Dormant. Some Lingering Branch Growth	None	Floral Branches Nearly Full Length. Buds Maturing	None
June	Dormant	None	Floral Branches Full Length. First Flowers Opening	None
July	Dormant	None	Flowering Well Started	None
Aug	Dormant Except for Some Branches After Heavy Rains	None Except in Exceptionally Wet Summers	In Full Bloom	None
Sept	Same as August	Same as August	Flowering Almost Completed	Ripening But None Ripe
Oct	Dormant	Same as August and September	None Except A Few Late Openers	Ripening and Starting to Fall
Nov	Dormant	Same as August and September	None	Maximum Seed Fall
Dec	Dormant	New Crop Forming May be Complete	None	None. Seeds All Shed

**Phenology*. The study of the sequence of seasonal changes in nature. All natural phenomena are included, seed time, harvest, flowering, ripening, migration, and so on, but often in practice the observations are limited to the time at which certain trees and flowering plants come into flower and leaf each year, and to the dates of the first and last appearances of birds and insects.

7

Germination and Establishment

Abundant seed production, rapid germination, and high viability would all seem to have high survival value in a xerophyte such as the boojum. In any event, the plant does possess all three in high degree. Although the thin seed coat permits rapid absorption of moisture and consequent rapid germination, this feature also makes the seeds highly vulnerable to seed-eating animals such as rodents, birds, and ants. These occur in abundance in the land of the boojum, and few seeds probably have the opportunity to remain around for more than one rainy season. For that matter, although we have not been able to collect any data on this point, it is probable that a vast majority are either eaten or stored away for later consumption even before the onset of their first winter's rains.

Despite extensive searching, very few seedlings have been found. The only ones that appeared to be less than one month old, and consequently could truly be classified as seedlings, were six that we observed in the Central Desert in late December after a period of good rains. Three months later, on our next visit to this area, none of these could be found. The vegetation and soil were thoroughly desiccated, and it may be assumed that the moisture that germinated the seeds was insufficient for establishment.

All indications point to conditions during approximately the first 30 to 60 days after germination making this period the weakest link in the life cycle of the boojum. The great numbers of seeds produced, their high viability, and rapid germination all are conducive to continued maintenance of the species provided conditions for establishment are favorable. They probably are favorable only at infrequent intervals, however, so that even though many seeds may germinate, few plants become established. Those that do manage to survive through their first few months would seem to have a reasonably high chance of developing to maturity.

Seed viability and germination

The seeds may remain highly viable for some time, at least under conditions of low temperature and controlled humidity. Seeds stored in one-pound coffee cans with plastic lids in a home refrigerator at an essentially constant temperature of 34 to 36 F lost none of their viability from October 1967 to April 1971. These conditions obviously do not prevail as features of the desert environment, and viability under field conditions may conceivably be relatively short.

Four separate germination viability tests were conducted at ambient light and room temperatures ranging from 63 to 68 F minima to 76 to 78 F maxima. In the tests, from 15 to 50 seeds were placed on germinating pads moistened with distilled water in petri dishes. Germination results are shown in table 7.1.

The above results, as well as those from other tests, indicate a rather wide variation in percent germination and apparent viability of the seed. This variability may be due, in large part, to the human factor involved in collection of the seeds used in the tests. For example, field trips were scheduled for periods when it was anticipated that seeds would be ripening. However, the peak seed production period could not be anticipated, and as a consequence degree of seed maturity and availability of fully ripened seed varied from year to year. Thus the 1967 seeds were fully ripe, while some of those collected the following year were not. These differences were reflected in subsequent germination tests.

Germination may also be affected by selection of the individual seeds employed in the tests. The seeds vary considerably in size, some having as much as twice the volume of others. The larger seeds tend to have a higher germinability than the smaller ones, in part, perhaps, because of a difference in degree of maturity. Consequently, unless exact size standards are adhered to in seed selection, the size factor will be reflected in the germination results.

When conditions are favorable, germination, as indicated by emergence of the primary-root tip, is rapid. A typical germination time-sequence test is indicated in the following notes:

February 29, 1968. 2:00 p.m. Placed 15 *Idria* seeds in petri dish on germinating pads wet with distilled water. Poured off excess water. Kept at ambient temperature and light. Temperatures varied between 75 and 80 F during the day and 60 to 70 F at night.

March 1, 1968. 8 a.m. Eight seeds germinated, none showing root hairs.

March 1, 1968. 5 p.m. Fourteen seeds germinated, 6 with root hairs.

TABLE 7.1

Germinability and viability of *Idria*

Seeds collected	*Date started*	*No. of seeds*	*Germination period*	*% Germination*
Oct. 1967	2/29/68	15	48 hrs.	100
Oct. 1967	11/26/69	50	144 hrs.	94
Oct. 1967	3/26/71	20	120 hrs.	100
Oct. 1968	11/14/68	50	36 hrs.	72

The 11/14/68 test was discontinued at 36 hours because all the ungerminated seeds had begun to mold and appeared dead.

March 2, 1968. 8 a.m. All 15 seeds germinated, all with root hairs.

Summarizing, it will be noted that 53 percent of the seeds had germinated after 18 hours, 93 percent after 27 hours, and 100 percent after no more than 42 hours (fig. 7.1).

Germination as affected by light

Germination may be affected to some extent by light. Two tests were conducted to determine a possible relationship between light and germination. Test No. 1 was run in a growth chamber under controlled temperature and light; Test No. 2 in an office under ambient light and temperature. All seeds were three months old and had been stored together in a refrigerator maintained at a temperature of 34 to 38 F.

Test No. 1: Ten *Idria* seeds were placed on germination pads moistened with distilled water in each of 20 petri dishes. Ten of these were then placed in a growth chamber at a constant 80 F temperature and alternating 12-hour light-dark conditions. The other 10 were placed in a similar chamber at the same temperature, but under constant darkness.

On the 7th day the dishes were opened and the germinated seeds counted with the results shown in table 7.2.

A t-test analysis of these data suggests a significantly higher variability and a lower proportion germinating at the 0.05 level of significance under light-dark conditions than under total darkness. However, some factor other than light or darkness is indicated because the variability recorded was almost twice the maximum theoretical variance. This other factor may have been the amount of moisture used to moisten the germinating pads, since each pad was thoroughly moistened but the amount of water used in each dish was not measured.

Test No. 2: Twenty *Idria* seeds were placed on moistened germination pads in each of two petri dishes. One dish was kept at ambient light

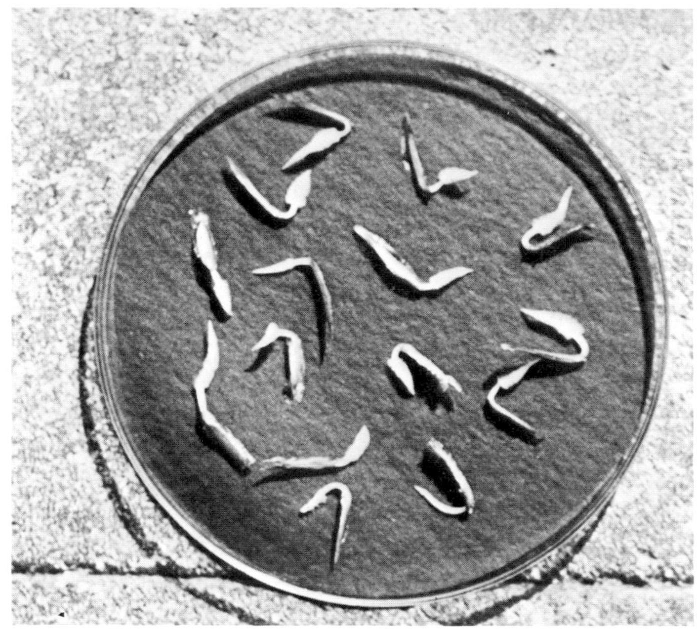

Fig. 7.1. Boojum seedlings 42 hours old. Primary root is densely covered by root hairs. Cotyledons have not yet emerged from seed coat.

conditions prevailing from November 29 to December 2. The second was wrapped in aluminum foil to provide total darkness. Temperatures for both ranged from night minima of 63 to 68 F to day maxima of 76 to 78 F.

When examined 36 hours after the test was initiated, 18 of the seeds under ambient light and all 20 of those in total darkness had germinated. This slight difference could have been due to inherent differences in seed viability and no significant treatment difference is indicated.

Seedling developmental characteristics

The rapidity with which the young plants develop is a critical factor in determining their ability to survive. Although it has not been possible to observe their rate of growth in the field, many such observations have been made on plants grown from seed in Tucson and elsewhere. Periodically recorded notes from one of the Tucson plantings, representative of the others, are given below.

November 7, 1967. Ten 2-day-old germinated seeds were transferred, one each, to circular, 4-inch-diameter plastic pots filled with soil dug from the surface inch beneath a nearby *Cercidium microphyllum.*

These were watered and placed outdoors in partial sun. Shade temperatures ranged from 50 to 80 F.

November 10, 1967. Three of the plants are emerging, though with the cotyledons still protected by the seed coat.

January 1, 1968. Although eight of the ten plants emerged and shed their seed coats in from three to six days, only three have survived. The others wilted and died, presumably from disease or desiccation. The remaining three have developed rapidly. Their growth is described below, at first collectively, later as *Cirio A*, *Cirio B,* and *Cirio C.*

January 15, 1968. Two of the three plants beginning to show side branches. Each plant has about 15 well-developed primary leaves, including the cotyledons which still persist in a completely green condition. One plant has side branches in the axil of every leaf including the cotyledons; one has a single branch emerging from just below the terminal bud; the third shows no sign of branching.

January 18, 1968.

Cirio A. Plant is now 40 mm tall to top of main stem. Has 13 leaves, all essentially mature. This includes the cotyledons, which are largely indistinguishable in size and shape from the others. Two branches developing, with primary leaves about one mm long. Main stem beginning to swell, suggesting its lifetime role in the storage of water.

Cirio B. Plant is 38 mm tall to top of main stem. Has 16 leaves, the two youngest of these about half-developed. No branches evident, although the stem is swollen.

Cirio C. Plant is 60 mm tall to top of main stem. Has 17 leaves

TABLE 7.2

Germination of *Idria* seeds in relation to light

	Number germinated	
Dish #	*Light-dark*	*Total dark*
1	4	8
2	5	9
3	7	10
4	7	9
5	7	8
6	9	8
7	8	7
8	6	10
9	9	9
10	2	10
Total	64	88
Average	6.4	8.8

including the cotyledons, the lower 12 of these with side branches starting. Leaves on side branches about one mm long. As spine formation in *Idria* is absolutely dependent on loss of primary leaves, and as all those plants still retain their primary (and only) leaves, none of the plants bears any spines.

February 26, 1968.

Cirio A. Main stem 40 mm tall, swollen. One side branch 33 mm long has developed vestiges of four other branches. Leaves all dark green and healthy.

Cirio B. Main stem 48 mm tall, swollen. No side branches, but vestiges of two showing. All leaves dark green and healthy.

Cirio C. Main stem 65 mm tall, swollen. Plant has brushy appearance with 12 side branches averaging between 20 and 30 mm in length. These have from five to ten leaves each [fig. 7.2].

June 5, 1968. All plants repotted in porcelain pots. When repotted they were set in more deeply than formerly, which affects height measurements from soil level.

Cirio A. Main stem 35 mm tall. Three branches, all leafless. Spines where primary leaves had been shed. Spines are slender, weak, but sharp and should provide fair protection. Main stem gray; not noticeably thicker than on May 1.

Cirio B. Stem 53 mm tall. Five branches, one with six primary leaves, one with seven, the others with none. Stem and spine characteristics as with Plant A.

Cirio C. Stem 55 mm tall. Twelve branches, all leafless. Stem and spine characteristics as with plants A and B [fig. 7.3].

February 15, 1969.

Cirio A, B. Alive, but leaves killed by freeze.

Cirio C. Killed by 22 F freeze of December 22, 1968.

April 6, 1971.

Cirio A. Alive, but leafless. 43 mm tall.

Cirio B. Dead; killed by January freeze of 13 to 15 F.

In summary: Five days after germination and three days after the germinated seeds were planted in soil they were emerging. In from three to six days most had completely emerged and lost their seed coats. After 38 days side branches were forming. By the 41st day the main stems had begun to assume the succulence that would characterize them the rest of their lives. Subsequently growth of the stem and branches continued. Except for partial loss of leaves when about seven months old as a result of desiccation, those plants that had survived the critical juvenile stage remained alive and vigorous until one died by freezing when one year and 46 days old, and a second by freezing when two years and 81 days old.

Fig. 7.2. Young boojum 113 days old.

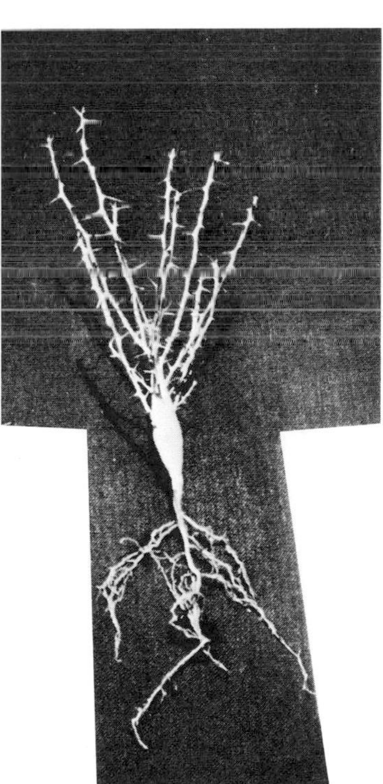

Fig. 7.3. Same plant shown in fig. 7.2 but 212 days old, showing complete root system, swollen main stem, method of branching, and spines.

Survival in relation to low temperatures

Idria will survive in temperatures much lower than those to which it is normally exposed. Although small plants have a higher mortality in subfreezing temperatures than larger ones, the minimum temperatures that either young or well-established individuals can endure is not known. However, several individuals three feet or more tall that have been transplanted to various locations in southern Arizona have survived for as long as 40 years. Five mature plants ranging in height from about five to 15 feet growing on the University of Arizona campus have probably been subjected to subfreezing temperatures for short intervals every winter since their introduction in 1929. None of them has suffered any apparent damage to the main stem in this period.

A short but valuable record of frost tolerance was obtained in Tucson during January 1971 when 20 cirios were exposed to temperatures as low as 13 F. These 20 plants ranged in size from one inch to 36 inches. Eight of the 20 were one inch tall, six were three inches, and two were four inches. In addition, there was one plant in each of the following inch-height classes: 8, 13, 15, 36.

Because the U.S. Weather Service forecasted abnormally low temperatures for the week beginning January 4, a hygrothermograph and max-min thermometer were placed in shade on the ground adjacent to the 20 cirios.

During the period January 4 to 11 all of the eight plants one inch tall were frozen solid each of the seven nights of record as well as several other times the same winter. During three nights when minimum temperatures of 13 to 15 F were recorded the eight plants in the three- and four-inch height classes were similarly frozen. The length of time they remained in this condition was not ascertained, but the thermograph record indicates several hours. There was also at least partial freezing of the plants eight or more inches tall but the extent of this was not determined.

Because temperatures as low as 15 F, and below-freezing temperatures for 12 to 20 hours may never occur in the boojum's native habitat, it might be assumed that mortality under these conditions would be high. Surprisingly, however, this was not the case. Only three of the 20 plants died and these were all in the three-inch class grown from seed planted two years previously.

Damage to the 17 survivors was slight and was restricted to the young, actively growing side branches and to the leaves. These new branches and their leaves were killed, as well as many of the leaves that had formed the previous summer. Except for temporarily affecting the appearance of the plants, this damage was of little consequence. By

Fig. 7.4. Boojum about 12 in. tall established in north-facing granite rocks.

April 1 most of the leaves had been replaced, many new side branches had developed, and most of the plants were starting to produce new terminal stem tissue.

Establishment in nature

Idria seedlings become established most commonly in one of three situations: (a) in rock crevices; (b) beneath the sheltering branches of low-stature, rather dense shrubs; or (c) in areas where small discrete rocks are lying on the soil surface.

Establishment in rock crevices

Establishment in rock crevices has been observed most typically and in the greatest detail in the Sierra Bacha, on the coast of Sonora. Establishment under these conditions, however, is not limited to this area, but also occurs in Baja California where similar conditions occur.

Conditions for germination and ultimate establishment appear to be distinctly unfavorable in the Sierra Bacha area. As a consequence, the species is largely restricted to slopes with a northerly exposure. Establishment, even in these sites, commonly occurs in crannies and crevices in the bedrock (fig. 7.4). These microhabitats provide relatively cool, shady conditions where evaporation and transpiration losses are reduced. At the same time they provide protection from potential enemies such as rabbits, rodents, birds, deer, or bighorn sheep. Because of the almost

Fig. 7.5. Mature boojum well-established on granite boulder near La Virgen.

vertical north-facing slopes where these plants often become established, some of them receive no direct sunlight in the late fall, winter, and early spring months during the first critical years of their lives. During this period the root system is developing and the stem is filling out and beginning to serve as a water-storage reservoir. Later, as the growing plant becomes exposed to sunlight and drying winds, it has established a protective covering of spiny branches, a usually adequate root system, and a fleshy main stem to store the all-important water.

Boojums often become established on what at first glance appears to be the smooth face of a granite boulder. This has been observed many times in Baja California, but most particularly in the Tinaja de Yubay area north of the abandoned Desengaño Mine site and the granite-boulder area near La Virgen.

Despite one's initial impression, the plants are not attached to bare rock surfaces, but are growing in cracks that provide a little soil and moisture and a rocky fortress against possible predators. Once established, the young boojums may live for an unknown number of years in these singular situations that provide not only physical protection, but, doubtless more important, a maximum of protection against evaporation of what is, at best, a meager supply of moisture. Figs. 7.5 and 7.6 show an old boojum growing on a granite boulder near La Virgen; fig. 7.7 a much younger, but still well-rooted, individual near Tinaja de Yubay.

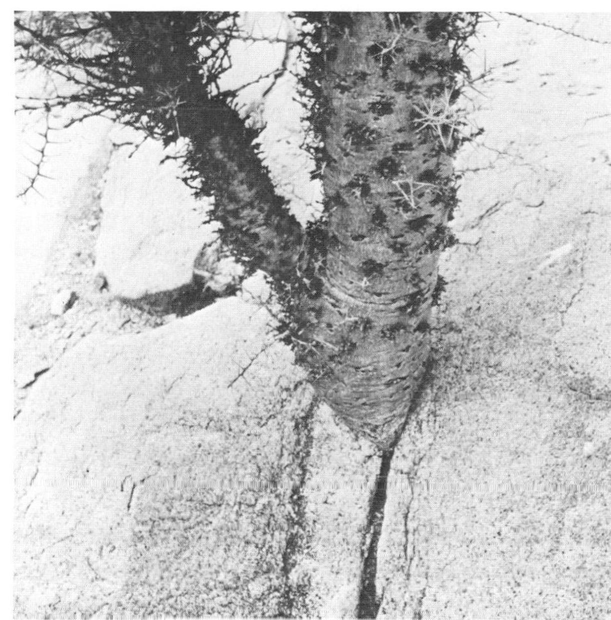

Fig. 7.6. Base of plant shown in fig. 7.5 showing slight crack in the rock that provides anchorage as well as a little moisture and soil.

Fig. 7.7. Young boojum flourishing in slight crack in granite boulder near Tinaja de Yubay.

Establishment beneath shelter shrubs

Establishment in the shelter of dense, low-stature shrubs is most typical of the various Baja California stands. In this connection, it is of interest that no small boojums have been found in the Sierra Bacha region growing beneath shrubs or on alluvial fills where such shrubs are most common. In Baja California, by contrast, the best sites, as indicated by density, size of plants, and rate of growth, are alluvial, usually sandy soils that support an abundance of shrubs. Even on these sites, however, only rarely are young boojums found beneath such larger woody species as mesquite, paloverde, ironwood, or other boojums. And this despite the fact that these larger species would seem to provide ideal conditions of shade, organic matter accumulation, and, particularly in the case of the boojum, protection from grazing animals.

The smaller shrubs, while usually providing a high degree of protection from foraging animals, have a lesser accumulation of organic matter than the larger, longer-lived species. They do, on the other hand, provide protection from animals and provide a fairly dense shade and windbreak, thus reducing both transpiration and evaporation.

On December 23, 1967, a total of ten man hours was spent searching for boojum seedlings in an attempt to determine the conditions under which they might have germinated and become established. The study site was 12 miles northeast of Punta Prieta on the road to Bahía de Los Angeles. Topography of this area is essentially level, the soil a uniform medium sandy loam. Both soil and topography are conducive to providing a uniform plant environment.

An area roughly 100 meters long and 50 meters deep along each side of the road was searched for the young plants. In order to be classified as "young" an individual had to have a stem height of 10 inches or less. Sixty-eight of these were found. Each was noted as to height, proximity to, and direction from other living and dead vegetation, and general growth characteristics.

Only three, with heights of three, five, and seven inches, were growing in the open and with no sign that they might have germinated and become established under the protection of either living or dead plants or other organic matter. Two of these had developed the coarse, scaly bark characteristic of older plants and appeared considerably older than others in their size class. They could, with a high degree of probability, have outlived any shrubs beneath which they might have germinated. The remaining 65 (96%) were associated with either living or dead vegetation of various sorts. In most instances they were growing within six inches of the main stem of a shelter plant; in all cases they were well within its branch spread and shade influence.

Ambrosia magdalenae was the most abundant plant in the area, consequently it is not surprising that most of the shelter plants were of this species. Rather unexpectedly, although there were many adult boojums that appeared to provide ideal shade, organic matter, and protection from foraging animals, not a single young boojum was recorded within the influence radius of these older individuals. Similarly, none was observed beneath *yucca valida* or mesquite, where both shade and humus appeared to provide excellent conditions for seedling establishment.

It appears highly probable that most, or perhaps all, of the boojum seedlings had become established beneath living plants. Seven of the nine seedlings with recorded heights of one to 1.5 inches, and that were classified as one year old or less, were growing beneath living *Ambrosia magdalenae* or *Eriogonum fasciculatum* bushes; the remaining two were sheltered by dead branches of *A. magdalenae.*

Almost half the 68 boojums observed were associated with dead remains of the original shelter plant. *Ambrosia magdalenae,* which provided cover 66 percent of the time, was also the only species in which a majority of the cover plants, 35 out of 50, or 70 percent, were dead. This would seem to indicate that *A. magdalenae* is relatively short-lived, at least in this particular habitat, or that mortality in the recent past had been abnormally high. The latter may have been the case since the precipitation record at Punta Prieta showed no rainfall during the seven months from January through July, 1967 (Hastings and Humphrey, 1969). Whatever the case, the associated young boojums were in all instances thriving. Many of them had actively growing branches with recently developed or still developing primary leaves.

Fifty-six of the young cirios were recorded with reference to direction from the shelter plant or plants, but no consistent directional relationship was observed.

A similar search made on March 20, 1968 in the Gold Mine Camp area, about 20 miles north of the previous counts, indicated the same relationship between *Idria* establishment and protecting overstory vegetation. At this location each of the young boojums recorded was small and appeared to have become established beneath the plant with which it was associated. One individual that was one inch tall was believed to be a 1966 or 1967 seedling. Eight were only two inches tall; one was three; two were four; one was five; and one had no height recorded. None was found in the open unassociated with other vegetation. And, as at the preceding Punta Prieta site, there was no apparent relationship between establishment and compass direction from the shelter plant.

The following day, March 21, 1968, an additional search was made for young boojums at Camp Víbora, a location about eight miles due west of Bahía de Los Angeles at an elevation of 1,400 feet. The soil here was a coarse sandy loam largely derived from granite. The richness and size of vegetation in this general area indicated a habitat highly favorable to the establishment and survival, not only of the boojum, but of a wide variety of associated species.

Although only five young boojums were found at this location during the hour that two of us spent searching, the field notes tell much the same story. As at the Gold Mine Camp site, no young plants were found in the open, unprotected by other vegetation.

Establishment between surficial small rocks

In those instances where *Idria* becomes established adjacent to small surface rocks, these seem to provide the modicum of protection from the elements and animals that permits the young plants to reach a size where they can survive. A few of the usually abundant seeds probably fall or are blown or washed into cracks in the soil adjacent to the rocks. Here, in the partial shade of the rock and its lesser evaporation rate than that of the open soil surface, a few seedlings survive. Mortality is undoubtedly high, but somehow enough plants do survive, even exposed as they are, to maintain the species.

Season of establishment

Boojum seeds will germinate at any season when there is abundant moisture for even 24 hours or less. It is possible, therefore, for germination to occur during either the summer or winter rainy periods. Despite this, however, and also despite the fact that occasional heavy summer rains may occur, it is believed that most of the seeds germinate during the late fall and winter, and that establishment may be restricted entirely to this period. These conclusions are supported largely by the time of seed ripening and dissemination, physical characteristics of the seeds, immediate post-germination characteristics of the seedlings, and the summer and winter climatic characteristics.

The seeds ripen only once a year, during the fall dry season just before the usual onset of the winter rains. They are thus available in maximum numbers during the fall and winter. They do not require a post-ripening period and have a thin seed coat, consequently are capable of germinating rapidly under adequate moisture conditions. Because they are not protected by a hard seed coat or other device against foraging insects, birds, or mammals, few of them probably escape for long being either eaten on the spot or stored for later consumption. Relatively few, therefore, remain for possible germination the following summer. The few that may start in the summer probably rarely, if ever, survive the scattered showers and continuous heat that characterize this time of year. Those plants that become established during the preceding winter-spring season, that have stored some water in their developing succulent stems, and thus survived the spring and foresummer drought, are able to replenish their dwindling water supply during the summer and so remain alive until the next period of winter rains. Summer for the would-be boojum would seem to be a time to refill its canteen and have a reviving drink, but not a time for initiating its long and droughty journey.

Climatic conditions during the winter are more conducive to establishment than during the summer. Winter temperatures are much lower during both the day and night, thus reducing soil evaporation and transpiration losses. Because of the lesser angle of incidence of the sun's rays insolation is much reduced, which also reduces evapotranspiration losses.

Individual winter storms are characteristically longer lasting than those of the summer, although the total precipitation during a given time period may be much less. Cloudy conditions with some precipitation may persist for several days at a time during the winter as contrasted with a few hours during the summer, providing conditions that are favorable for both germination and initial establishment. For ultimate establishment, it is probable that conditions enabling the soil to remain moist very nearly to the surface must prevail continuously for at least one month. As previously discussed in Chapter 1, this situation may never happen during the summer and only infrequently in the winter. The winter rains gradually taper off and often extend into March or sometimes April, thus extending the period when conditions may be favorable for germination and establishment. In contrast with the gentle nature of the winter rains, those of the summer fall as concentrated convection-type storms and as occasional torrential downpours accompanying the hurricanes that periodically sweep across the area. Storms of these sorts affect the precipitation means, but do not provide the long-drawn-out periods of cool-season moisture that favor establishment. In addition, the rains are not only concentrated within a short time period, but much of the water may be lost as flood runoff.

8

Local Habitat Requirements

The boojum is not restricted to any particular type of underlying rock, or to specific soils derived from particular kinds of rocks. Thus it shows no marked preference for areas underlain by granite, limestone, sandstone, basalt, or other rocks, or for the soils in which these rocks abound. No individuals have been found in markedly saline areas, an absence that could be due to the salinity, or because soils of this type tend to be poorly drained for extended periods.

Despite this catholicity with respect to substratum, the plants reach their greatest height and apparent maximum rate of growth in granitic areas. This may be because of the deeper, better-drained soils that characterize these situations rather than because of chemical differences in the rocks or their derived soils. Where, for example, the underlying rocks in adjacent areas change from granite to basalt, and the soils from coarse-textured granite derivatives to fine-textured clays, there is usually no discontinuity in the boojums but there are differences in size. Those on the coarser-textured soils are usually taller and less contorted, probably indicating more rapid growth.

Granite derivatives

One of the best boojum forests we have seen lies on a granite-derived soil, south of the Bahía de Los Angeles road and east of the San Borja turnoff before the Los Angeles road begins its descent to the gulf. Three other exceptionally good stands on granitic soils may be seen on the upland south of Arroyo de Calamajué and west of Sierra La Asamblea (see Gerhard & Gulick, 1967, Map 7), between San Borja and San Ignacito, and along the main road in the La Virgen-Santa Inés area. This last-named region, with its large granite monolithic boulders and rich vegetation, largely unspoiled by man or his livestock, could appropriately

Fig. 8.1. *Petrodromus* (rock mammal) and other granite monoliths with rich Sonoran Desert vegetation near Santa Inés.

be set aside as a national preserve against the day when the improved highway has been completed and "las turistas" find Baja (figs. 8.1, 8.2, 8.3).

Most of the boojums in the Sierra Bacha of Sonora are growing on soils derived from granite. Locally (see below under Basalt derivatives) they may also be found there on soils derived from fine-grained igneous rocks. Unlike the Baja California plants, those in Sonora rarely occur on coarse-grained valley alluvium, but are restricted almost entirely to small pockets of soil on the hillsides or to cracks in the bedrock on the north faces of the typically steep hills.

Basalt derivatives

Much of the Central Desert is underlain (or overlain) by fine-grained igneous basalts of more recent origin than the granites and older metamorphics. These basaltic flows appear to vary widely in age, ranging from perhaps Miocene or immediate post-Miocene time to the mid- or late eighteenth century when the Tres Vírgenes volcanic peaks were reputedly still active.

Fig. 8.2. Unique boojum tree habitat near La Virgen.

Fig. 8.3. *Yucca schidigera* in granite rock area near La Virgen.

Fig. 8.4. *Idria* growing on basalt hillside in south end of Sierra Bacha, Sonora.

The basaltic mountains, hills, and bajadas are so widespread in the land of the boojum as to make it difficult to select any for emphasis without, by implication, suggesting that others are less typical. More or less at random, therefore, I mention a few locations where the boojum may be seen in abundance and flourishing in the dry soils of basalt-strewn hills. One of the better stands occurs between Punta Prieta and Laguna Chapala; others may be seen between Punta Prieta and Rosarito, as well as between Rosarito and San Borja Mission, and at many locations along the side road to Bahía de Los Angeles.

Until recently the boojum population in Sonora was thought to occur in the Sierra Bacha only on soils derived from granite. The present study, however, has shown that the species grows equally well in restricted rhyolitic areas in the northern and central portions of these mountains. More recently we have found boojums thriving near the southern end of these mountains on basalt. Here, as elsewhere in the Sierra Bacha, they are restricted almost entirely to north-facing slopes. On these exposures, however, they are flourishing and reproducing, appearing on the whole as well adapted as they are elsewhere in the Sonora area. In this atypical location they are growing on the slopes of a basalt boulder-strewn hill about seven miles west of Rancho Coyote and immediately north of Arroyo San Ignacio (figs. 8.4, 8.5). This portion of the mountain range contains several isolated basaltic hills that contrast sharply with their matrix of lighter granite or alluvial outwash.

Fig. 8.5. Character of the terrain with basalt boulders in south end of Sierra Bacha, Sonora.

Limestone derivatives

We have found the boojum growing on limestone-derived soils only in one region, the area north of San Fernando between El Arenoso and El Progreso. Its presence at this single location does not indicate a lack of adaptability of *Idria* to limestone soils, but rather to the limited occurrence of limestone within its geographical range. In this rather limited portion of the Central Desert, the outcropping dolomitic limestone is visible as exposed folded strata in disjunct low mountain masses adjacent to the main road (fig. 8.6).

Although scattered boojums occur rather generally throughout these mountains, the mantle of soils overlying the rocks is usually shallow or lacking. As a consequence vegetation of any sort becomes established only with difficulty. At the bases of the steeper slopes where soils have developed and accumulated, the plant cover suggests no incompatibility between the soil and most species, including the boojum (fig. 8.7).

Soil reaction or pH value

Idria has been found growing on acidic soils only occasionally, occurring usually in moderately alkaline situations. Its more frequent occurrence on moderately alkaline soils is probably not because it is better adapted to these soils but simply because most of the soils within its range are alkaline.

Soil reaction was determined for 30 soil samples collected from 15 widely scattered locations and a variety of soils from 15 sites within the geographic range of *Idria* in Baja California and from six in Sonora. These have been classified as soils derived either from granite, from basalt, from dolomitic limestone, or from volcanic ash. In all except those derived from granite, they were underlain by varying amounts of caliche hardpan.

Of the 15 "Baja" sample sites, six had pH values that ranged from 8.0 to 8.4; four from 7.5 to 7.9; three from 7.0 to 7.4; and two from 6.3 to 6.8. Although boojums were visible from all the locations, they were not actually growing on all the collection sites. Their absence, however, probably cannot be attributed to the soil reaction, as the pH values where there were no boojums varied considerably (7.4, 7.9, 8.1, 8.2) and did not differ appreciably from the values of most of the *Idria*-supporting sites.

The tolerance of *Idria* for either extremely acid or extremely alkaline soils can be determined most effectively under controlled laboratory conditions. It was not the intent of the present study to determine these extremes, but rather to learn some of the pH values encountered in the field where the plant typically occurs. From these field data it may be

Fig. 8.6. Dolomitic limestone formation with thin soil mantle and little vegetation near El Progreso.

Fig. 8.7. *Idria* and other vegetation in limestone soils near El Progreso.

concluded that the usual habitat is neither strongly alkaline nor strongly acidic, but ranges commonly from slightly acidic to moderately alkaline. The data suggest further that a condition of slight to moderate alkalinity is more usual than one of slight acidity.

Soil texture

As has been indicated, *Idria* has an affinity for well-drained soils such as those derived from granite. On the other hand, although it shows a preference in fine-texture soil areas for the relatively well-drained hillsides, it also thrives on essentially level sites in some areas with moderately heavy soils, where drainage as a whole is poor. The main highway north of Punta Prieta passes through an area of this sort.

There is, nonetheless, an apparent limit to the lack of aeration that can be tolerated. In certain Central Desert localities the boojum communities have abrupt boundaries, where a mixture of species gives way suddenly to almost bare soil or to little vegetation except *Ambrosia camphorata* (fig. 8.8). Shreve (1951, p. 105) noted that this species was abundant on and "a sure indication of extremely fine volcanic clay."

The small size of the soil particles on these sites as compared with other basalt-derived clays on which *Idria* thrives is suggested by moisture-tension analyses at 15 atmospheres. The single analysis that was run on what we might term a "camphorata clay" gave a reading of 17.22 atmospheres. This contrasted with a range of from 4.69 to 8.21 and an average of 6.38 from 11 samples of volcanic clays supporting *Idria.* In further contrast, a granite derived coarse sandy loam recorded a moisture-tension of only 1.67 atmospheres. As a matter of record this same soil showed the following mechanical analysis percentage separations: gravel, 23.0; very coarse sand, 29.0, coarse sand, 28.33; medium sand, 9.70; fine sand, 7.41; very fine sand, 1.94; silt (through a 300-mesh screen), 0.62.

Soluble salts

Idria, like other flowering plants, has an upper tolerance limit for soluble salts, but this extreme has not been determined in the present study. Determination of the soluble-salt content of 11 Central Desert soil samples indicated a typical range from 189 to 910 ppm and an average of 522 ppm. Four additional samples collected within *Idria*'s range but on which no boojums were actually growing, ranged from 301 to 945 ppm with an average of 607 ppm. Although the salt content of these latter four is a little higher than that from soils supporting *Idria,* it will be noted that for the most part the analysis values overlap and do not indicate distinct salt tolerance levels. Despite this, they are of

Fig. 8.8. Fine clay soil supporting almost no vegetation in foreground, with better-drained, coarser-textured soil in background supporting a good stand of boojums and other vegetation. Site near El Arenoso.

value in providing data on the salt content of a variety of soils in which the plant grows. The soil samples used in these analyses were from the 15 sites tested in the pH analyses discussed previously, and consequently included a variety of soil types and a wide geographic range.

Direction of slope

The boojum is strongly direction-of-slope oriented in some geographic areas. This was first noted in the present study with reference to the Sonoran population, where most of the plants occur on northerly-facing slopes.

Slope relationships in Sonora

During August 1967 we recorded the relative abundance of *Idria* on opposing north-facing and south-facing slopes near Punta Cirio at the northern limits of the species on the Sonoran coast. Two sites were selected that were roughly equal in area and degree of slope and character of underlying rock, and that were representative of the general area with regard to boojum density. They differed primarily in that site A was north-facing while site B was south-facing.

Each boojum sighted was recorded with reference to direction of slope, not of the general area, but of the ground at the base of each plant. Because of surface irregularities this resulted in some plants with limited northerly exposures even on the south-facing slope and vice versa. Except for direction of slope, similarity of the sites was further assured in that both were located on opposite sides of the same hill. Exposure was recorded by compass to the nearest degree. For the purpose of this analysis, the data have been summarized into 36 groups of 10 degrees each, thus including all 360 degrees of the compass (fig. 8.9). A total of 310 boojums was recorded in this way on both areas, in addition to two on the level crest of the hill that were not included.

The compass was not adjusted for declination, thus the readings represent magnetic north and deviation from the magnetic pole. In interpreting fig. 8.9, the compass reading for a slope facing exactly north reads 180 degrees, and one facing exactly south 360 degrees. Thus NW-facing slopes include degree readings from 90 to 179; NE from 269 to 180; SE from 270 to 359; and SW from 89 to 360. Or, less specifically, slopes with a northerly exposure have readings from 91 to 270° while those with a southerly exposure read from 1 to 90° and 270 to 360°.

A study of the August analysis data, as shown in fig. 8.9, indicates a strong tendency for the plants to group in the 140 to 209° range or no more than 40° either east or west of the exact north facing reading. The northeast-facing slopes from 210 to 269° provide the most exten-

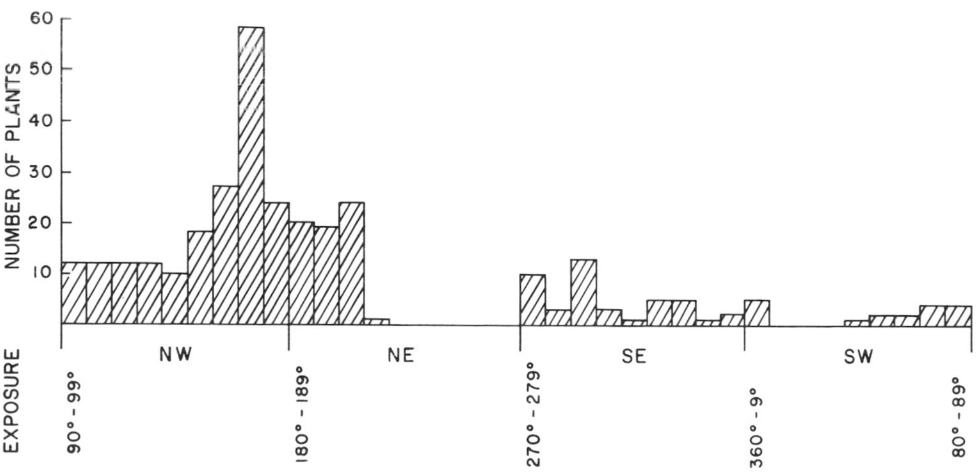

Fig. 8.9. Occurrence of *Idria* at Punta Cirio in relation to direction of slope.

Fig. 8.10. Boojums in the central Sierra Bacha area growing on a north-facing slope.

sive unfavorable exposure, considerably more so, in fact, than the southeast exposures, or, indeed, than most of the southerly exposures.

As a general conclusion, these data tend to corroborate the general impression that the boojums in this area occur primarily on north-facing slopes (figs. 8.10, 8.11). In addition, however, they also reveal more individuals than had been expected growing on both south and southwest exposures. Nonetheless, the total number of plants with a northerly exposure is five times that of all those with a southerly exposure.

The sites included in the above recordings were irregular in shape, consequently no attempt was made to determine their area as a basis for calculating plant density. Density data in relation to degree and direction of slope were obtained the following month on eight quadrats that are summarized in table 8.1.

These counts and measurements substantiate the general conclusions drawn from the August analysis. The September analysis included 87 plants on north-facing quadrats and five on south-facing. It will be noted that the boojum density on the north-facing quadrats varied from 28 to 52 per acre and averaged 33.8, as contrasted with the south-facing population that ranged from none to seven and averaged 4.7.

This ratio of seven to one is not markedly different from the less exact five to one ratio of the August analysis and, like that analysis, bears out the general impression one receives when traveling in the area.

In the vicinity of the Pacific coast, the prime boojum sites are on hillsides protected from the almost constant winds that blow during the daytime from the ocean to the land. The critical factor affecting establishment as related to slope in this region is believed to be that

TABLE 8.1

Slope-exposure, cirio-density characteristics at Punta Cirio

	Slope		*Area*	*Cirios per acre*	
Quadrat	*Direction*	*Degrees*	*Sq. Ft.*	*No.*	*Ave.*
1	N	35	15,000	29	
2	NW	17	17,500	52	
3	N	29	20,000	28	33.8
4	N	24	37,500	29	
5	N	33	23,000	31	
6	S	22	17,500	7	
7	S	19	17,500	0	4.7
8	S	22	12,500	7	

Fig. 8.11. South-facing slope with no boojums, opposite the north-facing slope shown in fig. 8.10.

Fig. 8.12. Coastal-type boojums on protected slope near Las Palomas.

of desiccation. Although the winds do contain considerable moisture, either condensed as fog or simply as high relative humidity, they rarely carry enough over a 24-hour period to keep the soil moist or prevent its drying. Consequently, the slopes that are so oriented as to receive some protection from the winds are the ones where the boojum occurs most abundantly. Indeed, the densest stands observed in all of Baja California, although comparatively limited in area, were in these near-coastal locations (fig. 8.12). Situations of this sort are principally east-facing, although the orientation varies depending on configuration of the coast and the effect of local topography on prevailing wind currents.

In an area about midway between Mesquital and Miller's Landing the boojums occur largely on north-facing slopes (fig. 8.13). Eight variable-plot quadrats (Grosenbaugh, 1952; Cooper, 1957) were run here, four on a north-facing slope, four on a SW-facing slope. Both sites had an outcropping bedrock of basalt and both had a slope of five to eight degrees. In areas of comparable size, the north-facing quadrats had a total population of 52 boojums, those on the SW-facing sites only four.

A pattern of generally deficient precipitation with the most extreme aridity during the summer months may be the principal reason for this orientation, the north-facing slopes providing the slightly less arid habitat. With no more than an eight-degree slope, any difference in aridity due to insolation would seemingly be slight. However, under extreme drought conditions, even slight differences may be critically important in determining survival or death of the small seedlings.

It might be expected that at the boojum's extreme southern range in the Tres Vírgenes Peaks area they would be restricted to the cooler north-facing habitats. This, however, is not the case. The plants occur here only on the highest peak, but have become established near the summit on all exposures. Because the peak is difficult to climb and study on foot, no counts or other measurements of the plants were made to determine relative abundance on different exposures. Inspection from the air, however, suggested that they reached their highest density on the southern exposures.

Fig. 8.13. Coastal-type boojums on north-facing hillside between Mesquitál and Miller's Landing.

9

Herbivores, Parasites, Man, Epiphytes, and Pollinators

Boojum seedlings and itinerant rodents, rabbits, birds, and insects

Few animals, vertebrate or invertebrate, seem to find well-established boojums much to their taste. During the first days of their existence, however, the young seedlings may have a host of enemies ranging from leaf-cutting ants and other insects to birds, rodents, and rabbits.

Establishment problems in the vicinity of Tucson, Arizona, although not identical with those in Baja California or Sonora, probably differ largely in kind. Germination tests at Tucson suggest that the life span of the average boojum seedling may be short indeed. Just how short and why is indicated in the following.

Between 9 and 10 a.m. September 14, 1968, 110 selected, apparently highly viable boojum seeds were planted in the desert soil within the confines of a 39 x 74 inches frame 12 inches high that was covered with a double layer of translucent pliofilm to provide partial shade. Two seeds were planted one-quarter inch deep at each of 55 locations uniformly spaced six inches apart beneath this canopy. From planting time until termination of the test, the soil was watered once to twice daily to prevent loss of seedlings from drought. Strips of white cloth one inch wide by ten inches long were hung around the frame at six-inch intervals to discourage birds and rodents.

By September 19 (11:30 a.m.) 62 seedlings out of a possible 110 had emerged. Observations made during the next 13 days tell the rest of the story:

Sept. 20, 8 a.m.	59 seedlings.	Some have been cut off by ants or other insects.
Sept. 21, 8 a.m.	54 seedlings.	Some wilted and dead, not from drought.
Sept. 22, 8 a.m.	51 seedlings.	Loss by insects cutting off plants and leaves.
Sept. 23, 8 a.m.	50 seedlings.	
Sept. 24, 5 p.m.	41 seedlings.	
Sept. 25, 8 a.m.	41 seedlings.	
Sept. 26, 8 a.m.	36 seedlings.	Some dug out by curve-billed thrashers or cactus wrens.

Sept. 27, 8 a.m.	12 seedlings.	Invaded during the night by leaf-cutting ants (*Acromyrmex versicolor*). Nest treated with chlordane but ants under canopy still active.
Sept. 28, 8 a.m.	4 seedlings.	Mortality from insect and bird damage.
Sept. 29, 9 a.m.	4 seedlings.	
Sept. 30, 8 a.m.	4 seedlings.	
Oct. 1, 8 a.m.	3 seedlings.	
Oct. 2, 8 a.m.	0 seedlings.	Killing agents unknown, but presumed to be birds or insects.

In a subsequent test at the same location 50 seeds were planted, one at each six-inch location. The objective here was to determine damage from insects alone. In order to exclude birds and rodents the frame was encased in one-half inch mesh hardware cloth extending to the ground. Seeds were planted October 2 at 10 a.m. and watered as before.

On October 9 the maximum number of germinated seedlings, 40, was recorded. After counting, the frame was inadvertently left off with the result that by 8 a.m. the following day the 40 plants had been reduced to 28. This mortality appeared to be due to bird damage.

Notes for the following day, October 10, read: 13 seedlings. Invaded by leaf-cutting ants. Some of the cut-off plants still lying on the ground, others being, or already have been, carried off. Chlordane applied as band around three sides of the plot.

From this time until a severe freeze the night of December 21 only two more plants were lost, one by wilting and one that was pulled up, presumably by a bird or rodent that got inside the screen.

In the September 20 test, none of the plants survived long enough for the stems to have thickened and so to have developed at least a modicum of resistance to insect damage. In the October 2 test, on the other hand, the stems of the 13 individuals that survived the October ant invasion were beginning to show some thickening 25 days after planting. This additional strength and volume may have helped them in resisting additional ant damage.

Once the young boojums have developed a thickened main stem and spiny side branches they suffer little damage. Those with a main stem even as little as one inch tall and about the thickness of a lead pencil are rarely harmed, even in an area with an abundance of cottontails *(Sylvilagus audubonii),* round-tailed ground squirrels *(Citellus tereticaudus),* and Harris antelope squirrels *(Citellus harrisii),* and, among many others, two species of birds, the curve-billed thrasher *(Toxostoma curvirostre)* and the cactus wren *(Campylorhynchus brunneicapillus).* These two are constantly investigating and probing the soil, presumably looking for insects but uprooting many young plants during their foraging. This more or less accidental uprooting occurs only where the plants are unprotected by rocks or other vegetation. Aside from this, the only observed damage has been the tip of an occasional branch nipped off, probably by cottontails.

The boojum and large herbivores

Although occasional desert mule deer *(Odocoileus hemionus),* pronghorn antelope *(Antilocapra americana),* and bighorn sheep *(Ovis canadensis)* roam in the land of the boojum, I have yet to see any signs of their browsing on either the leaves or the twigs of the cirios. The only grazing use observed has been on plants whose contorted tips when in bloom twisted down near the ground. In such instances the flowering branches and the blooms they bear are usually heavily grazed.

Because of the lack of water, few domestic livestock are run where the boojum grows, either in Baja California or Sonora. As a consequence no observations have been made on use of the species as forage by any kinds of domestic stock. Because of the spines with which the branches are liberally covered, however, even if the animals found the leaves and young twigs palatable, very little use could be made of them, even by goats.

The boojum and parasites

Only two species of insects have been seen as parasites of *Idria:* aphids *(Aphis* sp.) and a species of tussock moth (Liparidae). Of the two, the aphids are by far the more common, and have been recorded both in Sonora and Baja California. In Sonora we photographed them on the leaves (fig. 6.21); in Baja the only time we encountered them in abundance was in May 1971 in the area between Desengaño and Yubay. Here they occurred in swarms on the lee side of every boojum, flying up at the least disturbance but immediately returning to the protection from the wind afforded by the trunk.

The tussock moth was recorded February 15, 1970 on only a single tree near Punta Cirio in Sonora. Here there were many young caterpillars busily eating the leaves. Six of these were collected. They pupated during the period February 18 to 23 (fig. 9.1), all emerging as female moths two to three weeks later from March 7 to 10 (fig. 9.2).

Although no plants are known to parasitize the boojum, it seems probable that dodder *(Cuscuta veatchii)* may do so occasionally. The ranges of the two overlap, and *Cuscuta* occurs commonly over at least a part of this region. It has been observed on ocotillo *(Fouquieria splendens),* which suggests the possibility of its occurrence on *Idria.*

So far as known, the boojum does not serve as a host for any species of mistletoe, despite the prevalence of mistletoe throughout its

Fig. 9.1. Pupal cases of tussock moths attached to pruned branch of *Idria.*

Fig. 9.2. Female wingless tussock moths clinging to the pupal cases from which they have emerged. Until preserved in formalin three days later, none of these moths had moved from their original positions.

range. Two genera, *Phoradendron* and *Phrygilanthus,* occur, the first generally and the second locally within the range of *Idria,* but neither has apparently found the boojum acceptable. Both are parasitic on a variety of other species, which, because of their aromatic, often viscous sap, would seemingly provide a less suitable habitat than *Idria*. For whatever reason, however, the boojum has apparently been found unacceptable and so seems to have been spared the support of at least one uninvited guest.

The boojum and man

Throughout most of its range, the boojum is little affected by man, perhaps largely because of the aridity and remoteness of the area and its consequent sparse population. The greatest disturbance of the plants in their native habitat results from removal of the young individuals by tourists and professional nurserymen who bring them into the United States as ornamentals or for sale. Because of its relatively greater accessibility, the Sonoran colony is particularly subject to this kind of depredation and the more accessible areas have suffered considerably as a result.

During periods of extreme drought, the mature plants are reputedly sometimes cut down and chopped open to be used as food for livestock. We have never seen this done, and it would appear to be a practice not often resorted to.

The early Indians probably left the cirios rather severely alone, as they had no edible fruits and yielded little in the way of wood for fires or construction. By some tribes, at least, they were considered not only of little value even as firewood, but were believed in some way to be harmful. According to the Jesuit missionary Wenceslaus Linck, writing in 1762, "Except for a few cacti, all that is to be seen here is a plant called *cirio*. They are harmful and are so utterly useless as firewood that the Indians, who are always seeking some defense against the cold, will endure the lowest temperature rather than use these *cirios*" (Burrus, 1967, p. 46). Clavijero (1937) in his 1789 publication described it as useless even for firewood, although admitting that because of the lack of fuel it was burned at the San Borja Mission. In a footnote Burrus (ibid.) mentions that Clavijero elsewhere describes the plant as harmful: "plante nocive e stravaganti."

Even today, the Seri Indians living along the coast of Sonora have a superstitious fear of the boojum that may have been handed down from the earlier peninsular beliefs. Edward Moser, who, with his family, has lived among the Seris at Desemboque for many years, says that the Indians consider the boojum a bad plant. They insisted that a young specimen he had planted in his yard be removed, declaring its presence was responsible for a recent severe drought.

Because of the high water and low wood content of the plants, there is little or no possibility of their being used as firewood by the mestizos who live in the Central Desert today, even though they may retain none of the old superstitious respect for them. They can be used as firewood only after dying and then drying for many months. Even then the circular xylem cylinder provides little wood and burns too rapidly to make a satisfactory fire.

The xylem skeleton is sometimes used to make corrals, or to provide the wattle on which mud is plastered to construct the walls or roofs of dwellings. However, as material from trees that have died of natural causes is usually employed in these ways, the living trees are rarely damaged.

An unverified report indicates that the hollow woody cylinders of the boojum are currently being used in making candles. The trunks are collected and shipped to Ensenada or San Diego where they are cut up into four- to five inch pieces. The hollow centers are then filled with colored candle wax.

Most botanists have a feeling and an admiration for the boojum that is probably shared by few of the native residents, as indicated in the following incident translated from Martinez (1947):

> The devotion with which botanists view the cirios is not shared by the natives. The only use they see in it is to make soap of its ashes. This scandalized me and forced me to tell them almost reproachfully, that they ought to preserve and be proud of these treasures. They explained that they only used some of the old cirios and besides, the soap was made on a very small scale for only a few people who didn't bathe very often.

Such a use of the plant, if still current, could employ only the dried remains, and, even if some might be cut down with soap making in mind, must constitute so slight a drain on them as to be insignificant in the extreme.

Only modern man, with his need for reassurance and support in a harsh and lonely Catholic land, could make use of the boojum in his religion. Not that he feels a sense of reverence for the plant in so using it; on the contrary, it serves as any inanimate object might, in the construction of roadside shrines. Two of these, contrastingly different but each highly original in its way, are shown in figs. 9.3 and 9.4.

The boojum and epiphytes

Flowering plants

One could assume that in a desert such as that in which the boojum grows there would be few epiphytes. The assumption in this case would

Fig. 9.3. Wayside shrine near the abandoned gold-mining town of Calmallí. The main trunk of a boojum has been carved out to form a kind of living grotto.

Fig. 9.4. Roadside shrine about one mile north of La Virgen. The central part is made from the woody skeleton of a boojum, the upper part from a discarded automobile gas tank.

Fig. 9.5. Prickly pear *(Opuntia)* growing as an epiphyte on *Idria*. Accidental establishment of this sort from seeds, presumably dropped by birds, is rare. Photo from near Sauzalito Mine.

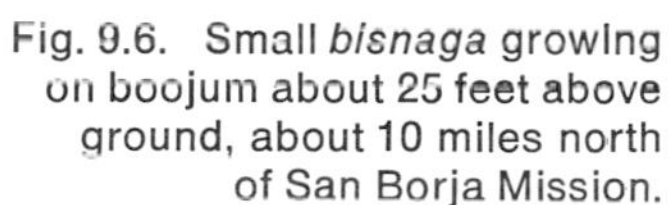

Fig. 9.6. Small *bisnaga* growing on boojum about 25 feet above ground, about 10 miles north of San Borja Mission.

be a sound one, for there is only a single species of flowering plant in the Central Desert that is known to grow as an epiphyte on the boojum, and none in Sonora. As will be seen, an occasional cactus may also be perched in strategic spots, as at branch junctures, but these are more accidents of nature than true epiphytes.

The only spermatophyte or seed-bearing plant truly epiphytic on the cirio is that unusual member of the pineapple family, Spanish moss *(Tillandsia recurvata),* more commonly known in Mexico as *heno pequeño* (little hay) or, north of the border, as ball moss (fig. 11.10). As this unique desert bromeliad is described at some length in Chapter 11, it is referred to here only in passing.

Two species of cacti have been seen growing perched on the boojum, prickly pear *(Opuntia* sp.*)* and barrel cactus or *bisnaga (Ferocactus* sp.*)*. Although well established, apparently for several years, these must have grown from seeds deposited in soil and debris that had accumulated in crevices or hollows high on the boojums (figs. 9.5, 9.6).

Fig. 9.7, 9.8. Witches'-broom type of abnormal branch growth on a boojum. Extreme proliferation may produce what appears to be an epiphytic or parasitic attachment.

Branching abnormalities that could easily be mistaken either for an epiphyte or for some kind of a parasite occur rather frequently on mature boojums. In at least one instance a growth of this sort bore a striking resemblance to a large swarm of orange-colored bees (fig. 9.7). Abnormal developments of these sorts appear to be an expression of extreme proliferation of the branch meristem (fig. 9.8). Although obviously not an epiphyte, this extreme proliferation could result from a virus or other parasitic organism affecting the meristematic branch tissues. In one instance most of the branches of the trunk were so affected (fig. 9.9).

Fig. 9.9. Witches'-broom affecting almost all the branches along the entire trunk of a boojum between Desengaño Mine and Yubay.

Lichens

Largely because of moist westerly winds from the Pacific, there is a wide variety of lichens that either encrust or drape the boojums in many parts of their Central Desert range. The most strikingly noticeable of these is a species which, paradoxically, is also dominant in the rain forests of the Pacific Northwest. Long streamers of the wraith-like *Ramalina reticulata* drape the cirios wherever they are particularly exposed to the moisture-laden Pacific breezes (fig. 9.10). At times the trees are so densely festooned that the branches and trunk are almost hidden, and seemingly smothered by the unbidden guest.

Ramalina may be seen, not only on the cirios, but on other woody perennials as well, *Pachycormus discolor* in particular, throughout much of *Idria*'s central range. Some of the heavier infestations occur east of Punta Prieta on the road toward Bahía de Los Angeles, between Marmolito and Rosarito and between Rosarito and San Borja.

The boojums growing near the Pacific coast are invariably lichen-bedecked, in some instances so densely as to make them appear at first glance to be in full leaf, or even to resemble a fir tree or some other species of conifer (fig. 9.11). At least one of the common species in these situations may be another *Ramalina, R. testudinaria* and/or *R. ceruchis*. Both of these occur commonly on a wide variety of habitats in the vicinity of the coast.

Fig. 9.10. Boojums near Punta Pricta draped with veils of *Ramalina reticulata. Machaerocereus gummosus* in foreground.

Fig. 9.11. Pacific coast boojum with no leaves, but covered with lichens. Near Punta Canoas.

Fig. 9.12. Gray-black coloration of *Idria* trunk, probably the result of some type of fungal growth.

Although the trunks of *Idria* are typically light yellow or gray or light green in color, not infrequently many of them in certain localities are dark gray to almost black (fig. 9.12). This coloration, although appearing to be a characteristic of the plant itself, probably results from a fungal covering. It does not appear to be a lichen (Thomson, 1971).

Other lichens growing on the bark of the tree shown in fig 9.13 were identified as *Caloplaca holocarpa, C. aurantiaca, Lecanora* sp., and *Anaptychia leucomelaena.* (Identifications by Canfield, 1971; Duewer, 1971; Thomson, 1971.)

A few other lichens were collected rather incidentally in the Central Desert on hosts or habitats other than *Idria.* These, as identified by Duewer (1971) and listed here as a matter of record, are as follows:

1. *Physcia aipolia* (Ehrh.) Hampe. On *Lycium* 10 miles east of Punta Prieta, B. C., March 21, 1968.
2. *Xanthoria polycarpa* (Ehrh.) Oliv. On *Lycium* 10 miles east of Punta Prieta, B. C., March 21, 1968.
3. *Xanthoria elegans* (Link.) Th. Fr. On *Viscainoa geniculata* and *Lycium* 8 miles east of Punta Prieta, B. C., July 31, 1968.
4. *Ramalina ceruchis* (Ach.) DeNot. On soil near Miller's Landing, B. C., March 29, 1968.
5. *Ramalina testudinaria* Nyl. On rock near Miller's Landing, B. C., March 29, 1968.

Pollinators

The boojum is pollinated, or at least the flowers are visited, by a wide variety of insects. As indicated in Chapter 4, these include moths and butterflies, bees and wasps, flies, bugs, and beetles. The flowers are also frequented by a species of spider, light-colored like the blossoms, that lies in wait for an unsuspecting victim.

Hummingbirds visit the plants not infrequently and may also be responsible for some pollination. Based on numbers and activity, however, it would seem that the various bees, wasps, butterflies, and moths are the chief pollinators.

Insects have been collected on the blooms during each of the four summers of this study. A partial list of bees collected in 1967–68 was published earlier by locality (Humphrey and Werner, 1969). In addition to the detailed list it was noted that:

> Various insects other than bees were taken on many of the blossoms, as would be expected. One of the groups most consistently represented in the Baja California samples was beetles of the family Melyridae, subfamily Dasytinae. What appears to be a single species of *Trichochrous* was present in many of the samples, sometimes in large numbers. Anthicid beetles of the genus *Ischyropalpus* and worker formicine ants were represented in several samples. Lycaenid butterflies and a skipper of the genus *Erynnis* were prevalent in the 1967 Sonora collections, and lycaenids were taken at two localities in Baja California as well.

In collecting the insects, no attempt was made to relate numbers of any species to area, i. e. to collect on a population-density basis. Despite an abundance of boojums in flower in all the collection areas, relatively few were within reach. Because a great majority of the plants in flower could not be reached, a traverse several miles in length, often over rugged terrain, usually had to be made to collect from even as few as five to ten plants. In some instances a single insect might be obtained from one plant, in others several might be netted. Because of these difficulties, it was not possible, or at least feasible, to attempt to make areal density collections.

Several variables affect the number of insects visiting any boojum at a particular time. The three principal ones seem to be maturity and number of blossoms, wind velocity, and time of day. The greater the percentage of flowers on a given plant that are in bloom, the greater will be the aroma given off by them to serve as an attractant. Related to this is the floral mass on a given plant, in that one with an abundance of floral branches is more showy and aromatic than one with relatively few branches.

Days with low wind velocities have consistently proven to yield more insects than those with higher velocities. Estimated wind speeds up to about ten mph seem to have little effect on insect numbers, but by the time they increase to as much as 20 mph there is a marked decrease in numbers. As wind velocities tended to be less in the early morning, the best collecting period was usually between 6 and 10 a.m. When there was a great deal of wind, even in the early morning hours, insect numbers were always down and collecting was poor.

Time of day, irrespective of wind velocity, also seemed to be a factor in that even in those days when wind velocities did not increase as the day advanced, there were markedly fewer insects available during the middle of the day and in the afternoon than in the morning. This may be attributable to temperature, since the plants bloom during much of the hottest part of the year, and the hot midday and afternoon temperatures may tend to discourage insect activity. They also may reduce the flowers' aroma, which could conceivably reach a peak during the night and early morning.

Insect collections through 1970, in addition to those published previously (Humphrey and Werner, ibid.) are summarized in Appendix B. The specimens are housed in the University of Arizona, Department of Entomology collection. In the Appendix, locations are shown only as Sonora or Baja California. For those who might wish more detailed data, each specimen label bears this information.

10

Some Community Relationships

This phase of the investigation had two primary objectives: (1) to obtain a quantitative expression of the perennial plants typical of that portion of the Sonoran Desert where *Idria* makes its home, and (2) to determine the major perennial species or taxa characteristically associated with *Idria* in various portions of its range in Baja California and Sonora.

General methodology

Three criteria were used in selecting study sites: (1) their geographical dispersion, (2) their variability with respect to habitat, and (3) the extent to which they represented both typical and atypical plant communities with *Idria* as a common species. They were not selected randomly or at specified distance intervals. This may suggest the possibility of bias or of errors due to selection judgement. These possibilities are conceded, with the defense that, considering the restricted time and funds available, the data obtained from a limited number of carefully selected sites would be more reliable than would similar kinds of data from an equal number of randomly located sites. A cluster-sampling technique was employed to assure that all sites were representatively sampled.

Plant composition and frequence were determined by recording the number of plants of each species encountered along a series of line transects.

The initial objective was to obtain both plant-composition and ground-cover data, employing the line-intercept method of Canfield (1942) and the modification of this method as developed by Strong (1966). Although extensive ground-cover measurements were made, they have not been included in the analysis. It was concluded that these measurements might be more misleading than useful because of the great variability in compactness and branching characteristics between species, and often between individual plants within a species. Because of this variability it was impossible to measure crown spread of some taxa in a way that would eliminate or even greatly reduce personal bias. Even in a measurement of the line intercept of grasses there is considerable room for bias; in most of the woody plants encountered in the present study the possibility of bias appeared to be so great as largely to invalidate any conclusions with respect to ground cover that might be drawn.

Examples of some of the more prevalent species with growth characteristics that make them more than usually difficult to measure include: *Machaerocereus gummosus* with its irregularly radiating arms and sprawling growth habit; *Agave shawii* and *A. deserti* with their tendency to grow as colonies whose formerly connecting stems may be dead or, if still living, are often buried beneath a mat of dead leaves that makes accurate determination of living plant area next to impossible; and *Fouquieria splendens* and *F. diguetii* with their slender, radiating branches. Even the common, less bizarrely branched shrubs and trees such as *Larrea, Prosopis,* and *Cercidium* typically do not form a closed canopy or a compact ground-cover unit.

Sonora analyses

Site locations

Two areas within *Idria*'s range in Sonora were selected for sampling. The first of these (Punta Cirio) was located near the northern limits of its range, the second (Punta Cuevas) lay about 12 miles to the south. Both were about a half mile from the coast (Map IV).

Four transect clusters or groups were recorded at Punta Cirio and five at Punta Cuevas. Each cluster consisted of ten 100-foot-long line transects placed ten feet apart. Because the boojums in Sonora are restricted largely to north-facing slopes, all the transects were located on slopes with either a northern or a southern aspect. All exposures had gradients of 20 to 30 degrees.

Punta Cirio. Three transect clusters were measured on the north exposure at Punta Cirio as compared with one on the south slope, thus providing some measure of variability in the first instance as well as providing a greater possibility of encountering the less frequent species in the second (Appendix C, tables 1, 2).* Because of the 3:1 ratio of clusters (and consequently of transects) neither frequence nor the total number of species encountered are exactly comparable on the opposing slopes. Despite this, it is of interest to note that on the combined north exposures there was a total of 27 taxa, consisting of 17, 23, and 15 on the various transect groups for an average of 18.3, only 2.3 more than on the single set of south-exposure transects.

---

*Because the rather numerous tables on which the discussion of plant composition in this chapter is based may be of interest primarily to the technical reader, they are given in Appendix C.

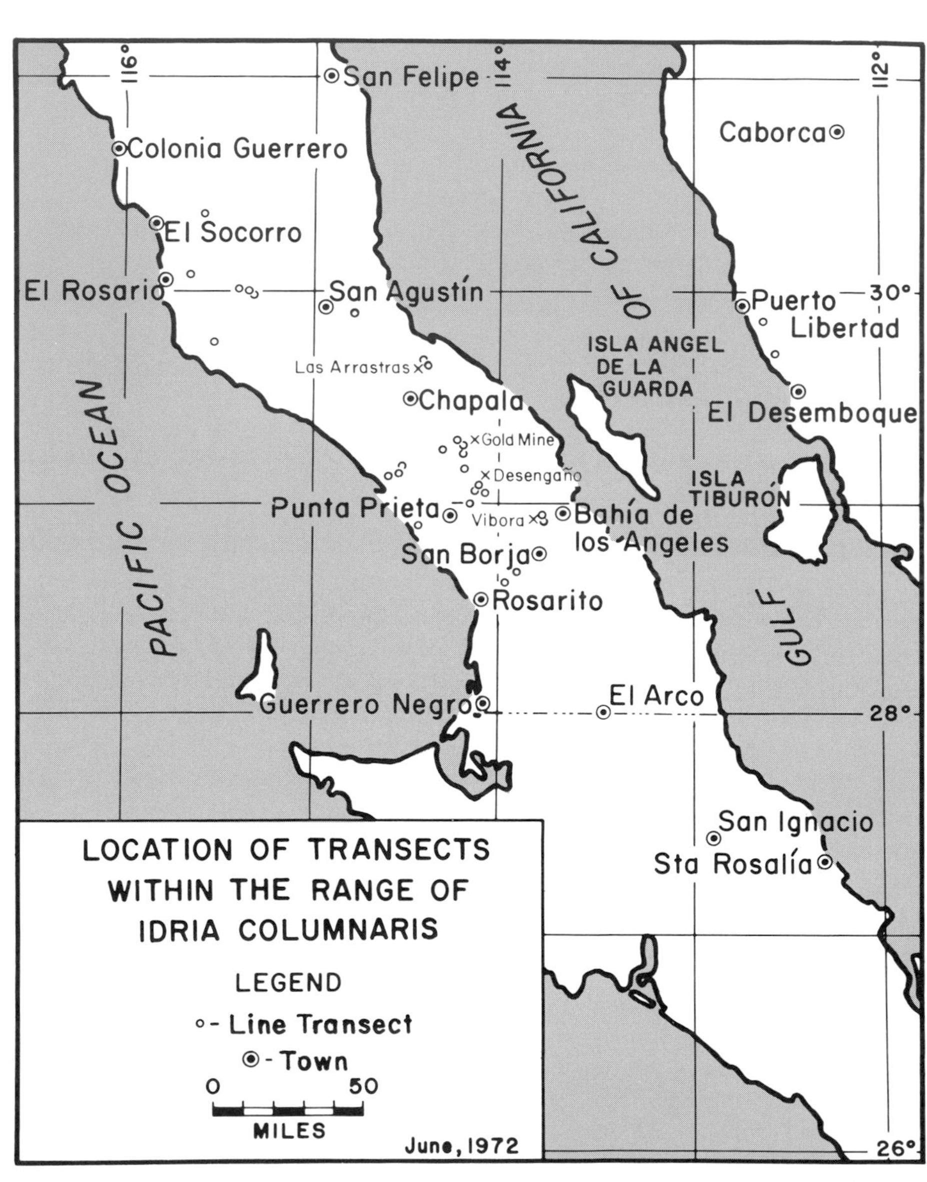

116°
114°
112°
30°
28°
26°
San Felipe
Caborca
Colonia Guerrero
El Socorro
El Rosario
San Agustín
Puerto Libertad
Las Arrastras
Chapala
ISLA ANGEL DE LA GUARDA
El Desemboque
Gold Mine
Desengaño
ISLA TIBURÓN
Punta Prieta
Vibora
Bahía de los Angeles
San Borja
Rosarito
GULF OF CALIFORNIA
PACIFIC OCEAN
Guerrero Negro
El Arco
San Ignacio
Sta Rosalía
LOCATION OF TRANSECTS WITHIN THE RANGE OF IDRIA COLUMNARIS
LEGEND
- Line Transect
- Town
0
50
MILES
June, 1972

Somewhat different frequencies (number of plants, as distinct from taxa) were found on the two exposures, the north-facing transect clusters recording 11.9, 20.9, and 15.5, with an average of 14.0, as compared with the single south-facing reading of 14.5.

The major vegetational differences between slopes are seen in the floristic details of the two habitats. Although the disparate numbers of transect groups prevent exact comparison of the numbers of species that were restricted to a single exposure, a group-by-group analysis indicates some major floristic differences. A comparison of Appendix C, tables 1 and 2, for example, shows only two species at Punta Cirio that were restricted to the south slope, as compared with 13 that were restricted to the north. On an individual transect group basis, we find that of these 13, six were recorded in only one group, three in two groups, while four occurred in all three. Of these four *(Idria columnaris, Larrea tridentata, Lycium californicum,* and *Solanum hindsianum),* only *Idria* has been previously mentioned by other workers as occurring primarily on north-facing slopes in this area. This may be because *Idria* is relatively conspicuous, rather than because the other species may not have the distribution differences suggested by these records.

Punta Cuevas. The opposing-slope data at Punta Cuevas lend themselves slightly better to comparison than those at Punta Cirio, since they consist of three transect clusters on the northwest exposures and two on the south. Here the number of species on the NW-facing slopes ranged from 15 to 23, with a total of 28 and an average of 19, and from 13 to 17, with an average of 15 and a total of 19 on the south exposure (Appendix C, tables 3 and 4).

Comparable opposing slope frequences ranged from 11.6 to 20.9 with a 14.6 average on the northwest exposures, and from 12.4 to 17.2 with a 14.8 average on the south.

Site comparisons

Analysis of the Punta Cuevas data indicates certain parallels with the Punta Cirio observations. Eleven species were restricted to the north- or west-facing slopes as contrasted with only one on the south-facing. This one, *Pachycereus pringlei,* was recorded only once, and, although not encountered on the transects, does occur on both slopes.

Of the species that were restricted to the northwest exposure, five were recorded on only a single cluster of transects, two were recorded in two clusters, and four in all three. Two of these last four, *Idria* and *Lycium,* also occurred on all the northern exposures at Punta Cirio. The two others, *Euphorbia misera* and *Ambrosia dumosa,* were recorded in two and three northern-exposure clusters, respectively, at Punta Cirio. The *Ambrosia* there, however, was not restricted to a single exposure.

As in most plant communities, a small fraction of the species accounted for a majority of the individuals encountered. On the north-facing slopes at Punta Cirio, for example, only four of the 27 species *(Encelia farinosa, Fagonia californica, Ambrosia dumosa,* and *Jatropha cuneata)* constituted 53 percent of the total. On the south exposure in the same area, two of the 16 species *(Encelia farinosa* and *Jatropha cuneata)* accounted for 59 percent.

Similarly, at Punta Cuevas, of the 28 species, the same four comprised 46 percent of all the plants encountered on the NW-facing slopes. Inclusion of the three next most abundant *(Bursera microphylla, Solanum hindsianum,* and *Sphaeralcea* sp.) resulted in seven species accounting for 70 percent of the total.

The sampling data obtained on these nine transect clusters are recognizably insufficient to provide a basis for a reasonably complete analysis of the floristics and plant frequence of the northern Sierra Bacha region. They do, however, constitute a partial quantitative basis for an analysis of composition and frequence in the ecosystem represented.

In order to obtain actual boojum densities,* a careful search was made for all the individuals growing within the perimeters of the areas sampled at Punta Cuevas. The results are interesting in that they show, perhaps even more clearly than the transect counts, the effect of exposure on the establishment of *Idria* in this area. The NW-facing slope shown in fig 8.10 had been selected primarily for its apparently good stand of *Idria* as one component of the vegetation, and the opposing south-facing slope shown in fig. 8.11 as a typical opposing habitat. The apparent suitability of the northwest exposure on the one hand to the establishment and survival of the boojum, and the unsuitability of the opposite slope on the other, are borne out by the two counts. The northwest slope had 37.7 plants per acre; the south slope none.

The region is floristically poor, as indicated by the fact that no more than 23 perennial taxa were encountered on any one of the 90 transects sampled. Plant composition tends to be rather consistent over the geographic range involved, as is shown by the general similarity of the species recorded at each site. A compilation of all species in the area would result in many more than were encountered on the transects, since the transects were restricted to hillsides supporting *Idria* or to opposing hillsides. Two types of sites, in particular, that are rather restricted in area are not represented: sand dunes and littoral areas. Both of these have a rather distinctive flora. Were they included, the number of species would be increased, but still would not result in a rich flora for the region.

---

*Density: the number of individuals per unit area.

Baja California analyses

Sampling techniques and site locations

Composition and frequency data were obtained from 26 groups or clusters of transects from selected locations within the range of *Idria* in Baja California. As indicated earlier in this chapter, these transects, like those in Sonora, employed a cluster-sampling technique and were located on a basis of geographical dispersion, habitat variability, and plant community similarities and dissimilarities. The objective in selecting locations was to obtain a wide range of each of these variables on sites supporting *Idria*.

From north to south the transects sampled areas from the northernmost known range of *Idria* near La Suerte at about lat. 30° 30′ N to about lat. 28° 30′ N, between Rosarito and San Borja (see Map IV; and maps 5, 6, 7, and 8 in Gerhard and Gulick, 1967). From east to west they extended from near the plant's most arid eastern limits between Bahía de Los Angeles and Molino de Lacy to within about five miles from the Pacific near Punta Negra, Las Palomas, and Boca de Marrón. All were located in areas that could be reached by car or rather readily on foot, consequently no data were obtained in the more mountainous, less accessible areas.

Twenty-two of the 26 transect groups consisted of ten equidistant, 100-foot-long line transects lying at right angles to a base line. On essentially level terrain the base line was randomly located; where extensive hills were sampled the base line was placed at the base of, adjacent to, and paralleling the base of the hill, thus permitting the individual transects to extend directly up the slope.

Two of the transect groups consisted of four 1,000-foot-long line transects in the form of a square, with the sides oriented due north, south, east, and west. A third group had a similar length and shape, except for the fourth side that fell in a radically different soil type largely devoid of vegetation and which, as a consequence, was omitted. Finally, one group consisted of three 100-foot transects that sampled a restricted area.

There was, thus, the equivalent of 43 one-thousand-foot line transects, and an additional three that were 100 feet long for a total of 4,300 feet of transects from the 26 locations.

Twenty of the groups were laid out on essentially level terrain with a slope of from zero to three degrees. The remaining six were on either north-, east-, or west-facing slopes of ten to 20 degrees, but in no instance were contrasting data obtained on opposing or adjacent slopes of different aspects.

A wide variety of underlying rocks and derived soils was represented in the sample areas. These were as follows: granite; basalt; basalt with volcanic ash and caliche; shale; deep, medium-fine sands probably underlain by granite; limestone; rhyolite; a granite-basalt mixture; and recent marine, semi-solidified sediments. In some situations a single group of transects was measured on a given one of these sites, others were sampled more intensively. The most intensive sampling was carried out on the better, more representative, *Idria* sites. In the discussion that follows, the data from apparently similar sites have been combined into a series of composite tables, each of which includes from one to ten transect clusters.

Coarse sand sites. Because, as indicated in Chapter 8, the boojum reaches its best development and greatest height on areas with coarse, sandy loam derived from granite, all of the transects that were located in such areas have been grouped in a single table (Appendix C, table 5). Species frequency data are here condensed from ten clusters, each consisting of ten 100-foot-long transects spread over three geographically distinct areas.

Soils analyses have not been run on all of the three sites. All, however, were classified tentatively as coarse sandy loam and appeared to differ little from each other. Consequently, a physical analysis of soil collected ten inches below the surface at the Camp Víbora site has been accepted as characteristic of all three. The analysis yielded the following size-class separates:

Gravel — 23.0 percent
Very coarse sand — 29.0 percent
Coarse sand — 28.35 percent
Medium sand — 9.70 percent
Fine sand — 7.41 percent
Very fine sand — 1.94 percent
Silt (through 300-mesh screen) — .62 percent

The soil texture indicated by this analysis suggests an area with little surface runoff, and as a consequence, with a high percentage of the precipitation absorbed by the soil. This apparently high infiltration rate is substantiated by the wide spacing and small size of the drainage channels or washes in all three areas.

Any interpretation of the relative abundance of plants listed in this and the other frequency tables should be tempered by a consideration of the recording technique employed in relation to the probability of encountering a particular species. Because the frequency figures represent chance interception along a line, it is obvious that the greater the crown spread of any individual, the greater is the possibility of interception. Consequently, species with short branches, as is the case with *Idria,* may be underevaluated, while the number of those with unduly spreading branches, as with mesquite and *pitáhaya agria (Machaerocereus),* may be exaggerated.

There is, however, a compensatory factor related to size, namely that large size inhibits the potential number of plants an area may support. As a consequence, relatively small plants with a lesser demand on space and moisture may be more abundant and thus have a greater likelihood of being encountered.

In the absence of any evaluation in this area of species frequence as affected by crown spread, the line-intercept technique here employed has been accepted as providing a reasonably reliable measure of relative species abundance.

Although 41 taxa in all were recorded on one or more of the ten transect clusters, 15 occurred only once in the entire group. As it has not been the purpose of this phase of the study to list all the plants that may occur associated with *Idria,* these 15 occasional taxa have been omitted from the tabulation. This has resulted in the omission of some usually common species such as palo verde *(Cercidium microphyllum),* ocotillo *(Fouquieria splendens),* and copal *(Bursera microphylla)* that do occur in the areas sampled. The effect on the mean frequency of omitting these low-density taxa is slight, or about half of one percent.

To the extent that these transect records correctly reflect plant frequency on deep sandy soils supporting *Idria* in the Central Desert interior, we may conclude the following. Three species are most abundant: the two densely branched, low-growing shrubs, *Ambrosia magdalenae* and *A. chenopodifolia;* and the leaf-succulent mescal, *Agave deserti.* These occurred on the average more often than any of the other 38 taxa, and, in addition, were recorded on from 50 to 90 percent of the ten transect clusters. The short-lived but perennial deervetch *(Hosackia glabra* var. *brevialata),* although apparently almost as common, was recorded on only three of the ten clusters, its average frequence being distorted by exceptional abundance at one location.

Next most abundant in the areas sampled were the giant maguey *(Agave shawii),* the slender, stem-succulent *candelilla (Pedilanthus macrocarpus),* and three nonsucculent shrubs, creosote bush, *tomatillo (Lycium),* and white bursage *(Ambrosia dumosa).* Others with almost the same likelihood of being encountered are the low half-shrub *Encelia californica,* the polymorphous boojum, the hard-stemmed shrubby *guayacán (Viscainoa geniculata),* one of the less spiny of the cholla cactus group *(Opuntia cholla),* and several other *Opuntia*s, including particularly the well-named and untouchable species that goes by the appropriate name of *O. molesta.*

All of the other species listed in Appendix C, table 5, and others that did not happen to be encountered, are characteristic of the same kind of habitat in the Central Desert. Their failure to be recorded here should not be taken as an indication that they may not be typical of other similar situations. Despite the 10,000 feet of line transect involved in these ten clusters, for example, no individuals of such to-be-expected species as foothill paloverde, *torote blanco, Jatropha cuneata,* or any of the *Viguieras* were encountered.

Shale-derived site. Immediately adjacent to the Gold Mine Camp granite-derived, deep-sand transects (Groups A, B, C, D of Appendix C, table 5), two additional clusters of ten 100-foot lines were run on a finer-texture sandy soil derived largely from shale. The results of these counts are shown in Appendix C, table 6. As only two sets of the transects totaling 2,000 feet were run here, as contrasted with four for a total of 4,000 feet on the deep-sand site, the total number of species on the two areas are not exactly comparable. It is of interest to note, however, that 22 taxa were recorded on the four deep-sand transect groups, and 27 from only two on the finer-texture shale-derived soils.

On each of the two transect clusters at the shale-derived site, there were 18 taxa; on the deep-sand site the number per cluster varied from 14 to 17. These are all extremely slight differences, which, although suggesting a slightly richer flora on the finer (and rockier) soil, are too slight to indicate significant differences between the two sites.

The relative frequencies of the few species at each site that are most abundant show some interesting similarities and, considering the fact that the two areas were adjacent and had similar slopes, some equally interesting dissimilarities. For example, on the deep, granite-derived soil *Ambrosia magdalenae* was most abundant, *Agave deserti* was second, *Ambrosia chenopodifolia* third, and *Hosackia* fourth. These totaled almost half the total recorded frequency, even though they represented only four of the 25 taxa.

On the adjacent shale-derived soils *Agave deserti* was most abundant with a 6.7 frequency, a figure that was higher than the total for the top four species on the deep sand. *Ambrosia dumosa* with 3.0 was second, a frequency that was greater than that of the total for the two most abundant species on the adjacent site. *Larrea tridentata* ranked third with .90, as compared with .49 and sixth ranking on the adjacent deep sand. *Ambrosia chenopodifolia,* the third most abundant species in the deep sand, was not even recorded on the shale soil site.

From this sampling intensity it is not possible to say that certain species were restricted entirely to either one of the two sites, but it seems questionable whether a complete analysis of both areas would reveal such a restriction. The sampling was designed primarily to determine relative abundance of the more abundant and characteristic taxa, and the fact that a few were encountered only on a single site was probably due to the sampling intensity.

Cerrito Blanco volcanic-ash. Four clusters of ten 100-foot transects were located about three miles northwest of the Gold Mine deep-sand and shale sites (Map IV). All three sites had a similar topography and elevation, differing primarily in soil characteristics. Because of proximity to the Cerrito Blanco ranch, these clusters are referred to as the Cerrito Blanco group (see Map 7 in Gerhard & Gulick, 1967). This area was selected for study because the vegetation, although containing a few boojums, appeared to be relatively sparse, growing in a locality characterized by considerable amounts of light-colored volcanic ash underlain by a highly alkaline caliche hardpan, thus providing soil conditions that were distinctly different from those of most *Idria* sites. The principal species encountered here, and their relative abundance are shown in Appendix C, table 7.

A comparison of plant composition on this site with that of either the preceding Gold Mine Camp deep sand or shale sites reveals no appreciable difference in either total frequence or number of taxa. Twenty-eight in all were encountered for a total frequence of 11.3 per 100 feet of transect.

Initial scanning of the transect data indicated that a large majority of the taxa were encountered only occasionally, and that a small percentage accounted for most of the record. Ten occurred in only one of the four clusters, eight being encountered on an average only .025 times per hundred feet. These, *Acacia greggii, Aristida* sp., *Cardiospermum corindum, Condalia spathulata, Galium* sp., *Gutierrezia* sp., *Opuntia* sp., and *Yucca valida,* because of their incidental occurrence, have not been included in table 7.

Only three of the remaining 18 species, *Ambrosia chenopodifolia, Agave deserti,* and *Eriogonum fasciculatum* averaged more than one occurrence for every hundred feet. Of these three, *Ambrosia* was a strong numerical dominant with 4.15 hits per transect as compared with 2.40 for the second-ranked *Agave* and 1.10 for *Eriogonum.*

One species encountered here, winterfat *(Eurotia lanata),* merits special mention. Although not one of the most abundant plants, it was conspicuous throughout the volcanic-ash area and may be largely restricted in Baja California to this and similar arid sites characterized by an extremely fine-texture, light-color volcanic ash, or to areas with these physical characteristics combined with a high soil alkalinity, a characteristic that has been previously noted in the United States (Dayton, 1931, 1937). I have seen it locally abundant on similar soil conditions in the semi-arid West from Washington to Arizona.

In view of the close proximity of this volcanic-ash site to the granite- and shale-derived sites, it is interesting to note that several of the most abundant species on one or both of these areas were not recorded on the volcanic ash. For example, on the granite-derived deep sand four species — *Encelia californica, Ambrosia magdalenae, Lophocereus schottii,* and *Lycium* sp. — occurred in all four transect clusters. On the shale-derived soil, *Ambrosia dumosa* was recorded in both clusters and was the second most abundant species. None of these five was recorded even once in the 4,000 feet of transect on the volcanic-ash site.

Idria, although found in all three situations, appeared to be poorly suited to the relative aridity of the volcanic-ash. On both the granite- and shale-derived soils it occurred in all the transect clusters, with a respective frequency per site of .24 and .40. In contrast, although it was recorded in three of the volcanic-ash clusters, in each instance only one individual was encountered in every 1,000 feet of transect for an average per 100 feet of .075.

Although the soil in this area was roughly classified as a volcanic ash, a laboratory analysis indicated additional intrinsic characteristics. The prevailing caliche hardpan close to the surface suggested an alkaline situation; this was borne out by a pH value of 8.4. The soil had a moderately fine texture, as indicated by a moisture tension under a 15-bar pressure of 8.21.

It is obvious that these qualities represent only two of several that characterize the site. And neither the alkalinity nor the fine texture appear to be so extreme as to prevent establishment of most of the plant species growing in the general region. The extensive caliche, however, would largely prevent moisture penetration and make the area sufficiently arid to severely restrict seedling establishment.

Both the deep-sand and shale-derived soil sites were without caliche, and, particularly in the first of these two, the highly permeable soil was highly absorptive, permitting retention of most of any rain that might fall.

El Arenoso camphorata clay. A series of three clusters of ten 100-foot transects each was located two miles north of El Arenoso adjacent to and on the west side of the main road. The site was selected because it supported a good stand of *Idria* on a red clay soil derived from basalt. The terrain where the samples were obtained had a gentle slope ranging from about two to ten degrees, in part to the south, in part to the east.

The plan here had been to lay out four 1,000-foot-transect clusters as a square, as had been done twice before. However, by the time the fourth side was reached it was seen that if the square design were adhered to most of the fourth-side clusters would fall in an atypical, lower-lying, poorly drained area almost devoid of vegetation. As a consequence, this side was omitted, resulting in three clusters and a total of 3,000 feet of transect.

The soil throughout the area consisted of the peculiar red clay designated earlier as camphorata clay, because it constitutes the almost exclusive habitat for *Ambrosia camphorata.* In contrast with the poorly drained area, the upper, better-drained portions supported a wide variety of plant species, probably because of better drainage on the higher-lying, steeper gradient, and consequent more favorable soil aeration. Similar sharply contrasting vegetation differences that may be correlated with drainage are not infrequent on clay soils in this portion of the Central Desert.

Although no soil was collected at this particular site for later analysis, a collection was made at a nearby similar location from the vegetation-deficient component. This analysis indicated a pH value of 7.4 and a 17.22 moisture tension under a 15-bar pressure. This moisture tension, when compared with the 1.67 value obtained in the sandy soil at Camp Víbora, suggests that *Idria* may be well-adapted to an extremely wide range of soil textures except where drainage is poor.

A total of 29 plant species was recorded on the three El Arenoso transect clusters. Four of these — *Dalea emoryi, Encelia farinosa, Fouquieria splendens,* and *Trixis californica* — were numerically unimportant, occurring in only one of the three clusters and then only once in the entire 1,000-foot line. Densities of the remaining 25 are summarized in Appendix C, table 8. Many of these, however, are also inconsequential, in that they contribute little to the total composition.

Of the 25 species included in Appendix C, table 8, six — *Agave deserti, A. shawii, Ambrosia camphorata, A. chenopodifolia, Encelia californica,* and *Eriogonum fasciculatum* — comprise almost 75 percent of the total composition. None of the others occurred often enough to characterize the community taxonomically. One of the numerically dominant six, *Ambrosia camphorata,* is unique in that not only was it the most abundant single species recorded, but it occurred on none of the 25 other transect clusters. It should be noted, however, that none of the other transects was located on the type of fine, red clay that characterized this particular site.

San Fernando limestone and rhyolite. Aside from local onyx and recent littoral calcareous deposits, we have encountered extensive thick-bedded limestone in only one area of the Central Desert. Sedimentary deposits of this sort make up the greater part of the hills north of El Progreso and the old San Fernando Mission site. Igneous deposits, including rhyolite, are interspersed with the limestone.

Two transect clusters, each consisting of ten 100-foot-long transects, were located on a bajada at the base of one portion of these hills. The transects, one group on a limestone-derived soil, the other on one derived from rhyolite, were adjacent to each other, but separated by a narrow wash. Fragments of limestone were mixed with the soil on the limestone site, and of rhyolite on the rhyolite site. In each instance, the higher-lying bedrock consisted solely either of rhyolite or limestone, with no apparent possibility of intermixing of the parent material.

There was a 90-degree difference in direction of slope of the bajadas, the limestone cluster facing west, the rhyolite facing north. Both had an eight-degree gradient.

The general objective of making a vegetational analysis in this area was to determine whether (a) limestone affected the distribution of *Idria,* and (b) there were appreciable differences in plant composition on soils derived from limestone and rhyolite.

As indicated in Appendix C, table 9, three species, *Encelia californica, Eriogonum fasciculatum,* and *Ambrosia chenopodifolia* were numerically dominant on the limestone site, comprising 82 percent of the frequence recorded for the 14 taxa. These same three, with the addition of *Ambrosia magdalenae,* were also most abundant on the rhyolite site, accounting for 88 percent of the composition for the 13 taxa there represented.

A study of table 9, although indicating a number of slight differences in composition, reveals only one species that appears to be markedly affected by the site differences. It will be noted that *Ambrosia magdalenae* was entirely absent from the limestone area, yet comprised 41 of the 161 plants encountered on the rhyolite. Although this may have been due to difference in direction of slope or to other factors, there is a strong indication that the comparative alkalinity suggested by the limestone site may have adversely affected establishment.

Although four plants of *Idria* were recorded on limestone and none on rhyolite, this indicates a relative rather than an absolute difference. A count of all the boojums growing within the equal-size areas represented by each transect cluster showed 58 plants per acre on the limestone and a little less than half as many, or 24 per acre, on the rhyolite. At very least, one fact is evident: a limestone substratum and a limestone-derived soil have no apparent restrictive effect on the establishment and survival of *Idria.*

El Ciprés granite. A single transect cluster was located near the northwestern limits of *Idria* about 28 miles east of El Socorro. The cirios at this location were restricted to a small area roughly 1,000 feet long by 25 feet wide. The entire area was sampled by twenty 25-foot-long transects that paralleled each other at 50-foot intervals. They lay at an elevation of 2,100 feet on a 3 to 5 degree, south-facing crest of a round-topped ridge.

Although this area lies within the Sonoran Desert, it is approaching the Sonoran Desert-Chaparral transition and contains comparatively few species that are typical of the desert proper. The primary objective in locating a series of transects here was to obtain plant composition data on an area that supported *Idria* near the northwestern upper limits of the species.

Only 12 taxa were recorded on the transects (Appendix C, table 10). Of these, four predominated: *Agave deserti, Eriogonum fasciculatum, Ambrosia chenopodifolia,* and *A. magdalenae,* comprising 90 percent of all the plants encountered. These same species were also usually abundant at most of the lower-lying Sonoran Desert *Idria* sites. Others, such as *Larrea tridentata, Ambrosia dumosa,* and *Encelia californica,* that tended to characterize the lower-lying, more southerly sites, were conspicuously absent here. This absence, however, may have been due to the local habitat and may not have been typical of the general region. *Agave shawii* was also not recorded on the transects. This was undoubtedly an expression of the local habitat, since this mescal species occurs conspicuously throughout most of the adjacent area.

The only species encountered here that was recorded at no other locality was the wild rose, *Rosa minutifolia.* Although recorded only once on the transects, this small prickly rose occurs as the principal plant in much of this region, particularly on north- and west-facing slopes.

Agua Dulce granite. A single transect cluster was located about seven miles southeast of San Agustín near the abandoned Agua Dulce ranch (see map 5 in Gerhard and Gulick, 1967). An extensive area beginning about here on the north is characterized by a wide variety of shapes of large monolithic granite rocks and supports a rich variety of Sonoran Desert vegetation. Some of the more conspicuous plants are the *copalquín* or *torote blanco,* unusually tall boojums, and the cardón cactus (Humphrey, 1970, 1971).

The sample at this location was located on a ten-degree, south-facing slope. It consisted of ten 100-foot-long line transects spaced at 50-foot intervals perpendicular to a base line. The plants encountered are summarized in Appendix C, table 11.

Study of the table reveals several species that suggest a particularly arid site, a characteristic that might have been due either to the southern exposure, to a shallow soil, or to both. *Ambrosia dumosa,* an extremely drought-tolerant species, was numerically dominant, followed closely by *Agave deserti.* Three other extreme xerophytes, *Eurotia lanata, Gutierrezia bracteata,* and *Psilostrophe cooperi,* encountered rarely or not at all on the other transect sites, were also common here.

Despite the occurrence of *Idria, Pachycereus,* and *Pachycormus* in the general area, none of these was intercepted by any of the transects. The relative abundance of the first two, the boojum and cardón, tend to be overestimated in most casual observations because of their relatively great height. And, as was pointed out earlier, because their branches cover a comparatively small area, they are less likely than many other species with a similar density to be intercepted in line-transect sampling.

Las Arrastras clay. This site, which lay about seven miles northeast of Chapala, was selected because it appeared to represent a low-precipitation, high-temperature habitat near the northeastern limits of the boojum. The terrain was essentially level, sloping about one degree to the south. The soil, a fine clay that tended to crack on drying, was apparently derived primarily from basalt. Two soil samples collected here showed an average moisture tension of 6.24 under 15 atmospheres pressure, and a very slightly alkaline pH value of 7.6.

The boojums in this colony are relatively short, suggesting a slow rate of growth. They are isolated from adjacent stands, none being known to occur within a distance of about five miles.

Most of the boojums here occur in three rather discrete groups within a half-mile radius. Because of their isolation and apparent smaller-than-average size, the height of most of those in the area was measured. Sixty plants in all, ranging from three inches to 24 feet, were included in this analysis, and were classified on a basis of the heights shown in table 10.1.

As pointed out in Chapter 6, the maximum height of the boojum varies from one portion of its range to another. These differences are so great, yet so consistent, as to suggest the occurrence of distinct populations (Humphrey & Humphrey, 1969).

Except for the abnormally short plants at several Pacific Coast locations, both maximum and average heights of the Las Arrastras plants are consistently and markedly shorter than those at any other observed location.

The two tallest plants of the 60 recorded at the Las Arrastras site measured only 24 feet, and only four of the 60 exceeded 20 feet. Yet, as

TABLE 10.1

Boojums classified by height, Las Arrastras study area

Height class in feet	*No. of plants*	*Percent of total*
0 to 1.0	7	12
1.1 to 5.0	18	30
5.1 to 10.0	12	20
10.1 to 15.0	13	21
15.1 to 20.0	6	10
20.1 to 24.0	4	7
Total	60	100

determined by flowering and seed setting, 58 percent of the plants were mature. These growth data all suggest either a distinct low-stature population that has evolved through time in an isolated location, or a group of plants not genetically distinct but dwarfed by an abnormally harsh environment.

The size breakdown shown in table 10.1, despite suggesting environmental stress, indicates a stand that is maintaining itself. Five of the seven plants in the zero to one-foot category were less than six inches tall. And, a total of 42 percent that were five feet tall or less also suggests a vigorous and reproducing, rather than a decadent, stand.

In the plant composition analysis, a single species *(Atriplex barclayana)* comprised 93 percent of the total plants encountered in 2,000 feet of line transect (Appendix C, table 12). Despite this, because of the much greater size of the other species, the area gives the impression of an extremely open, medium-stature shrub community.

Although only a single boojum was recorded on one transect cluster and none on the other, a careful search revealed a total of nine within the area sampled by cluster A and 16 within the cluster B area for an average of 12.5 individuals or 7.7 per acre. Thus, the general floristic poverty of the site is expressed also by a sparse stand of boojums.

The total of only ten taxa correctly indicates the floral poverty of this and similar nearby clay-soil sites. The plants listed represented most of the species on these sites in the area, since a careful search revealed only three additional species: *Lophocereus schottii,* a very spiny, arborescent *Opuntia,* and a small *Mammillaria.* A check list made on an adjacent granitic coarse-sand site totaled 22 species, most of them with an apparent biomass much greater than that of those on the clay soil. One exceptionally tall ocotillo *(Fouquieria splendens)* on the granitic sand reached up to the record height of 26 feet, 3 inches.

San Ignacito basalt. Two transect clusters were located on basalt-derived soils between Rosarito and San Borja. These sites were selected because they were several miles from other transects, and the area they represented was extensive and contained a typically good stand of *Idria* and other species.

Soils in this general area, as on the transects, are derived largely from basaltic rocks, the remains of which still characterize the region as prominent, isolated, dark-colored conical hills and mesas. Except for the steeply sloping sides and pediments of these hills, the gradient in the general area ranges from almost level to about a three-degree slope on the bajadas. Slope on the transect clusters was insignificant, varying from one degree on cluster A to level on cluster B.

The 25 taxa encountered here suggest that the plant species on the basalt-derived low-gradient soils in the interior of the Central Desert do not differ outstandingly from those in other extensive portions of the region (Appendix C, table 13). And, as with the other sites, that only a few species account for most of the vegetation. Eight of the taxa were encountered only once per 2,000 feet of transect, four only twice, and two only three times. Deleting these as inconsequential or trace species reduces the total more typical taxa to 11. Of these, only seven were recorded on both transects. These seven — *Agave shawii, Atriplex julacea, Ambrosia chenopodifolia, Idria columnaris, Machaerocereus gummosus, Opuntia cholla,* and *Pachycormus discolor* — also characterize and are numerically dominant over other very extensive portions of the Central Desert.

As in several of the other transect clusters, all the boojums were counted that fell within the area sampled. Twenty-seven were so recorded on cluster A and 37 on cluster B, for an average of 38 per acre.

Arroyo del Rosario basaltic clay. Ten transects were located near El Rosario on an essentially level plateau 12 miles from the Pacific. This location was selected as representing a habitat close enough to the ocean to be affected by it, yet far enough inland to have the coastal climate considerably modified. Although the vegetation appeared to be more representative of the interior desert than of the coastal region, no quantitative floristic data were available to serve as a basis for an exact description of the plant cover.

The plant composition in this area, as indicated in Appendix C, table 14, is distinctive primarily for its floristic poverty and for a high percentage of cacti falling within two genera, *Machaerocereus* and *Opuntia*. As is the case with much of the Central Desert, *Ambrosia chenopodifolia* was found to be the numerical dominant. Although only two boojums were intercepted by the transects, not only is the species abundant throughout the general area, but, as throughout its range, the wide variety of sizes encountered indicates a reproducing population well-adjusted to the extremes of a harsh environment.

Pacific Coast. Five areas, all five miles or less from the Pacific Coast, were sampled. The northernmost of these was located five miles from the coast near Cajiloa, about 25 miles south of El Rosario, the other four between Las Palomas and Punta Negra some 25 to 30 miles further south (see maps 5 and 7 in Gerhard and Gulick, 1967). Because of their geographic isolation and apparent soil and floristic differences, the Cajiloa transects have been analyzed and discussed as representing one distinct area (Appendix C, table 15). The other four clusters, all within a 20-mile radius and equidistant from the coast, have been summarized as a group in Appendix C, table 16.

The Cajiloa transect cluster lay on a uniform slope of about two degrees to the west. The underlying rocks were calcareous, semiconsolidated sedimentaries overlain in part by a clay loam with transported alluvial quartzite pebbles.

The prime reason for sampling the vegetation at this location was that it supported a stand of *Idria* not far from the Pacific Ocean, and that a considerable distance separated the site from any of the other areas sampled.

Study of Appendix C, table 15 suggests that the species characterizing the Cajiloa portion of the coast may not differ appreciably from those of the interior. The only species abundant here that had not been previously recorded is *Ambrosia bryantii.* In this instance, it was not only present, but made up almost a third of all the plants encountered. This abundance often characterizes this particular plant, which tends to grow in large numbers on some clay sites. Its predominance here is probably due to local soil conditions and/or a comparatively high relative humidity; it does not indicate any unusual tendency for it to be restricted to the Pacific coastal region.

Pacific Coast — Las Palomas to Punta Negra. Transect clusters A and B of Appendix C, table 16 were located less than a mile south of Las Palomas on a 15 to 20 percent north-facing slope. Each consisted of ten equidistant 100-foot line transects for a combined transect length of 2,000 feet. Both were located on a rocky clay loam overlying metamorphosed basalt.

Although the taxa encountered on each were not identical, it will be noted that the totals were the same; also that these totals were twice those on the two other coastal transect clusters included in the table. Of interest also is the fact that the 16-taxa totals for clusters A and B are identical with the number of taxa encountered on the Cajiloa coastal group of Appendix C, table 15.

Except for *Aesculus, Frankenia, Myrtillocactus,* and *Xylonagra,* the taxa listed in the two Las Palomas transect clusters also occur commonly in the interior of the peninsula. These four, on the other hand, are all either exclusively or primarily restricted to coastal areas, and all except *Frankenia* occur only on the Pacific slope.

Aesculus parryi grows rather commonly throughout the range of *Idria* near the Pacific, usually extending inland for about five miles. *Frankenia* has been recorded over much the same north-south range, but occurs as a numerical dominant on both sides of the peninsula. And, where *Aesculus* is found most typically on the hillsides, *Frankenia* is most at home in poorly drained, low-gradient swales or bajadas. (In contrast with this typical distribution, however, note its abundance in cluster D of this table.) *Xylonagra,* a sparsely branched, shrubby member of the primrose family (Onagraceae) has been recorded inland for about ten miles and is seemingly best adapted to hillsides and the banks of washes. *Myrtillocactus,* with its attractive candelabra-type branches, has never been encountered by us more than about five miles from the Pacific coast.

The two most abundant species recorded in the Las Palomas area, *Eriogonum fasciculatum* and *Ambrosia chenopodifolia,* are also often numerically dominant in the interior on a wide variety of sites. This is true also of several other taxa, including *Agave shawii, Encelia californica,* and *Euphorbia misera,* that were recorded frequently on these transects.

Cluster C was located four miles south of Las Palomas on a very gently sloping bajada with a rocky clay soil overlying basalt. The site was selected in part because it was typical of extensive areas near the coast where *Frankenia palmeri* and *Atriplex julacea* predominated. It will be noted that this apparent dominance was borne out by the transect measurements — these two species accounting for 83 percent of the total frequence for all eight taxa.

Two species, *Dudleya acuminata* and *Frankenia palmeri,* were particularly characteristic of this slope, comprising 87 percent of the total plants recorded for all of the eight taxa encountered. *Xylonagra* was also more abundant here than on most sites; otherwise the species were those common to many inland areas.

Overview

Ninety-nine taxa in all were recorded on the 16 transect clusters in Sonora and Baja California (Appendix C, table 17). This represents somewhat less than an equivalent number of species, since 16 were classified only as to genus, and, in some instances, as for example *Dudleya, Lycium,* and *Opuntia,* more than one species was recorded within a genus.

Although 33 taxa were intercepted by the transects in Sonora as compared with 90 in Baja California, this in no way indicates the relative richness of the flora in the two areas. Not only were there three times as many transect clusters on the peninsula, they were also distributed over a much wider area. Both of these factors would favor the chance interception of more taxa in Baja California.

Twenty-four taxa occurred on both sides of the gulf. It will be noted that seven of these (excluding *Idria*) — *Eriogonum fasciculatum, Euphorbia misera, Fouquieria splendens, Ambrosia dumosa, Larrea tridentata,* and *Simmondsia chinensis* — not only were encountered frequently on both sides of the gulf, they also were recorded more often (8 to 10 times out of a possible 20) than any other taxa. They might, therefore, be considered as the outstanding numerical dominants among all the taxa of record. Three others, however, *Encelia farinosa, Ferocactus acanthodes,* and *Lophocereus schottii,* met the same distributional criterion and were encountered almost as often.

Idria was also recorded in a large majority of the clusters in both locales. This, however, was not a chance occurrence as it was with the other taxa, since its presence was a prerequisite for site selection.

It will be noted that one large family of plants, the grasses or Gramineae, is almost entirely lacking in both the Sonora and Baja transects. A single perennial grass plant was intercepted on the entire set of transect clusters. It had been obvious throughout the study that grasses were poorly represented over the entire geographical range of the boojum. The extreme poverty of this representation is emphasized by the single interception.

The Sonoran Desert is typically an area characterized by shrubs and low-stature trees. Some drought-resistant grasses are often a minor component of the vegetation, and may be common on certain sites as, for example, in swales or on clay-soil sites where *Hilaria mutica* or *H. belangeri* sometimes form almost pure stands, or in some of the desert wash or dune-sand areas of southwestern Arizona, northern Sonora, and Baja California that provide an excellent habitat for *H. rigida.*

Climatic conditions under which the boojum can germinate and become established are apparently highly unsuitable for the survival of grasses. Most of this area receives little or no grazing by livestock that might tend to overgraze grasses and thus inhibit their establishment or persistence. In the absence of destructive grazing, it must be concluded that some natural components of the ecosystem preclude grass establishment.

The variety of soils encountered, some of which appear to be well-suited to grasses, would seem to rule out the possibility of soil as the ultimate grass-limiting factor. Climate is thus left as the prime, or more probably the only, limiting factor. And, of the various aspects of climate, the extended and not infrequent periods of no effective rainfall are believed to be critical. The woody plants, either through their succulence and consequent ability to store water, or their extensive and deep root systems, often combined with highly effective leaf and stem phenological characteristics, are able to survive where the grasses are not.

11

Selected Associates of the Boojum*

Roughly 230 miles south of the International Boundary in Baja California begins what may easily be the most fascinating desert of the world. Variously known as the Vizcaíno Desert, the Vizcaíno Region (or Province), the San Borja Desert, and the Central Desert, it continues for some 300 miles to the southeast.

Physiographically the Central Desert is not particularly exciting, consisting, as it does, largely of gently sloping upland with scattered hills and low mountains. If not exciting physiographically, however, it has many features that are both scenic and interesting. The Arroyo or Cañon de Calamajué, for example, with its perennial stream of mineralized water and the slate-blue to gold-and-red canyon walls is enough to make almost anyone feel that the rough travel was at least partly justified. Or the recently active Tres Vírgenes volcanic area, with its difficultly accessible summit and extensive lava flows that look as though they might have cooled only yesterday. Or for those with the ability and the facilities, the rugged mountains and deep canyons of the Cerro San Francisco, site of the Indian petroglyphs described by the late Erle Stanley Gardner in *The Hidden Heart of Baja.*

The first thing that strikes the eye, though, is the queer assortment of plants and their size and abundance. When we were first exposed to this desert some years ago, even though we had lived in the southwestern Arizona desert for many years, we were quite unprepared for what we saw — the giant cardón cacti, the grotesquely fat elephant trees (often completely shrouded in orange-yellow dodder), the tall and almost stately or oddly contorted boojum, and the brightly scarlet-flowered false mesquite seemed too unreal to be true. Then, and even today, we feel that we went down a rabbit hole and came out into an Alice-in-Wonderland world.

---

*Reprinted with modifications by permission from *Cactus and Succulent Journal.*

In our study of the cirio or boojum and its associates, we have come to feel an empathy for this Central Desert and its varied forms of life. We are getting to know it and its plants and animals in many of their moods and at all seasons of the year. A few observations on some of the more common or unusual plants follow.

Agave shawii

Various species of *Agave* in Baja California, as elsewhere in Mexico, are commonly known as *mescal* or *maguey*. As the term *mescal* is applied typically to the species used in distillation of the alcoholic beverages mescal and tequila, other species are commonly and more correctly known as *maguey*.

Typical plants of *Agave shawii* often seem to be readily distinguishable from other members of the genus. At other times they are difficult to separate from other species, *A. deserti* in particular, with which *A. shawii* often grows intermixed. As Wiggins (in Shreve & Wiggins, 1964) indicates: "The range of variation within a species is often extremely puzzling, and it is probable that hybridization occurs frequently."

Agave shawii is the largest and one of the most commonly encountered members of the genus in the Central Desert. Despite its size and the fact that it is one of the so-called "century plants," the individual rosettes probably do not usually exceed an age of 15 to 20 years (Shreve, 1951).

Each of the species of *Agave* in the Central Desert is interesting in its own way, but none is quite as eye-catching as *A. shawii* (fig. 11.1). Several features make it outstanding, most of them related to its size. Towering above the other *Agaves*, the flowering stalk may reach a height of 15 feet. This elongating stem more nearly resembles a giant stalk of asparagus than anything else that comes to mind. The heavy stalk, which may be three to four inches in diameter, has no true leaves, although it does bear widely spaced stem-hugging leaf scales. As the stem shoots up, the flower-bearing branches develop in the axils of about the upper half of these scales. These branches elongate rapidly as the main stalk reaches its full height, finally ending as dense clusters of greenish-yellow to orange flowers pollinated by bees or other insects, hummingbirds, and bats.

Although the flower stalk is the most spectacular feature of the plant, the rosette of large basal leaves in which the stalk is centered is also strikingly attractive. The numerous heavy, bright-green leaves range up to about five inches wide and 20 inches long. They are well-protected by a single strong sharp spine at the tip and by other vicious-looking spines along their margins.

In a land where there are few trees and little to use as building materials, the large straight maguey stalks find ready acceptance as a

Fig. 11.1. *Agave shawii* in full bloom.

sort of substitute for logs. As logs go, they are neither large nor durable, but are easy to collect and serve as a foundation for mud-plastered walls, as corral reinforcing, and to make short stretches of fence around homes and garden plots. When green and in the bud or early flower stage, the developing stalks are cut and used as feed for livestock. This always seems such a waste of the years of growth that each stalk represents, but man and his hungry animals have no sympathy for the reproductive effort of one maguey.

Pachycormus discolor

Certainly not as bizarre as the boojum, but by most standards more beautiful and as interesting, *copalquín,* also known as *torote blanco* and as elephant tree, gives a uniqueness to the Central Desert that is not exceeded by any other plant. It branches more or less like an orthodox tree, but in spite of this manages to have a most unorthodox appearance (fig. 11.2).

The *copalquín,* which may have more than one stem from near the ground, branches in the apparently haphazard manner of many trees to form a rounded crown generally from 15 to occasionally as much as 30 feet tall. The trunk, at three to five feet above ground, may be as much as three feet in diameter and almost throughout appears swollen and turgid to the point of being grotesque. As the stems branch, they taper very rapidly, which further adds to their heavy, fat appearance.

The bark is smooth, even on the large trees, and tends to peel off in thin yellow-white sheets rather like the exfoliating bark of some birch trees. As they are leafless much of the year, the light-colored trunk and branches are usually not hidden by leaves and give a clean, striking appearance, especially when seen in the light of early morning or late afternoon.

In addition to having a contorted, sometimes grotesquely elephantine appearance, the *copalquín* is strikingly handsome at all seasons, although presenting markedly different seasonal aspects, beginning in April and May when the leaves are turning yellow and dropping, through the fragrant pink glory of its blossoming in June, July, and August; to its white, barebranched nakedness in times of drought or its green phase when clothed with an abundance of new light-green leaves after the rainy season.

The name *torote* means "big bull" and refers to the plant's heavy, supposedly bull-like appearance. "Elephant tree" was obviously similarly

Fig. 11.2. Elephant tree showing typical branching habit.

inspired as was the generic name *Pachycormus,* "pachy" from the Greek meaning thick or stout, and "cormus" meaning stump or log. The specific name *discolor* refers to the plant's tendency to have two rather distinct colors of flowers; one almost white but with a slight touch of pale pink, the other a definite pink or light rose. The flowers on individual trees are largely either one color or the other, offhand giving an appearance of two different species.

The durable *torote blanco* is amazingly adaptable in its ability to grow under widely differing climatic conditions. Although typically a resident of the hot, dry interior, it will grow, as it sometimes does, on the Pacific coast, where cool winds from off the ocean blow almost constantly and where the high nighttime, and sometimes daytime, humidity and fogs are commonplace. If appearance is any indication, it endures this kind of climate and adjusts to it, although with difficulty.

In the interior the name *torote blanco* aptly fits. On the coast, by contrast, it resembles and could much more correctly be called *la foca,* the seal. Here it often lies prostrate on the ground as a response to the constant winds, little resembling the typical stalwart inland form (fig. 11.3).

The overall attractiveness of the tree is enhanced by the setting where it often makes its home. Although by no means restricted to sites with a coarse, well-drained soil, some of the best specimens do grow in such habitats. I have in mind particularly areas such as that between San Augustín and Cataviñá on the main highway south of El Rosario. This is a region of enormous granite boulders eroded into surprising shapes and interspersed with a rich combination of Central Desert vegetation.

The largest individuals we have seen occur in the relatively recent lava flows south of the Tres Vírgenes volcanic peaks near El Mezquital. It was here that one tree near our camp had a measured height of 30 feet and a diameter three feet above ground of 30.5 inches. Such heights are atypical and seem to indicate an unusually favorable environment.

Pachycereus pringlei

Probably the best way to describe the cardón to those familiar with the cacti of Arizona is to say that it resembles an enormously heavy sahuaro (fig. 11.4). Particularly when young, before the large side branches develop, there is a close similarity to the sahuaro. With maturity and increasing age, however, the two become increasingly dissimilar. The name "cardón," by which *Pachycereus pringlei* is almost universally known in Baja California, is also applied to other large cacti of Mexico. The same term is used as well for teasel or thistle, and presumably refers

Fig. 11.3. Pacific coastal form of the elephant tree hugging the ground to escape the prevailing, salt-bearing westerly winds.

Fig. 11.4. Unusually tall cardón near Tinaja de Yubay.

to the prickly fruit, particularly that of *Pachycereus pecten-aboriginum,* whose bristly fruits have long been used by the Indians as hair brushes.

The distribution of the cardón and sahuaro is interesting in that both find conditions to their liking over a considerable portion of the coastal area of Sonora, where their ranges overlap for a distance of almost 200 miles. Although the cardón is abundant in the Central Desert, there is no sahuaro there or indeed anywhere in Baja California. What has kept it from somehow becoming established on this peninsula during the millenia that it must have been flourishing a short distance to the east across and near the head of the Gulf of California? Or, by the same token, why has *Idria* remained restricted to its limited range for perhaps an equal length of time? Seeds of the sahuaro are eaten by birds, doves in particular, and it would seem that they must have been dropped many times on fertile ground across the gulf. The boojum, whose seeds are wind-borne, has managed to establish only one outpost in the Sierra Bacha area, south of Puerto Libertad, Sonora, 75 miles from the nearest Baja California stand on Angel de la Guarda Island.

One would not have to be aware of the cardón's generic name *(Pachycereus)* to see a strong resemblance between the basal portion of its trunk and the leg of an elephant. Although the cardón trunk is the larger of the two, it has the same solidity and spreads out a little as it enters the ground, much like the toes of an elephant. Both are thick, fairly smooth, and gray.

Shreve (1951) says the cardón may reach heights of 50 to 60 feet. Moran (1968) describes it as reaching heights of 50 or "perhaps even 70 feet." Although we have not made a consistent search for abnormally tall individuals in Baja California, we have measured occasional plants that appeared unusually tall. Thus far we have found none that measured more than 48 feet. This is about as tall as the sahuaro which may reach a height of 50 feet.

The cardón has its greatest thickness near the ground, in contrast with the sahuaro which usually reaches its greatest diameter more than halfway to the top. And, where the sahuaro increases gradually in diameter from a relatively slender base of five to 12 inches, the cardón stands solidly with a massive 20 to 36-inch spread (fig. 11.5). (Moran [ibid.] cites a five-foot maximum diameter.) The massive trunk and the heavy branches, many of which originate near the ground, give the cardón an impression of durability, great weight, and an age greater than that of the sahuaro. Which of the two has the longer life span no one knows, but I would hazard a guess that it is probably the cardón.

It would seem plausible to expect that the cardón and the sahuaro, since they look much alike and are closely related, would bear similar

Fig. 11.5. Characteristically thick base and low branching on an old cardón.

fruit. For whatever reason, however, the fruits are rather dissimilar. Those of the cardón resemble a large chestnut burr that splits open when ripe, showing a purple-red or white, moderately fleshy interior (fig. 11.6). The sahuaro, by contrast, has a sparingly spiny fruit that splits open at maturity to expose a bright red, juicy, fleshy mass surrounding shiny, black seeds. The sahuaro fruits are highly edible and have long been sought after not only by the Indians and later settlers of the Southwest, but by birds, ants, coyotes, and other animals. The comparatively dry cardón fruits have some food value, but except for the small black seeds, which are eaten by birds and ants, would seem to be so unattractively packaged as to repel rather than attract most potential foragers except perhaps a hungry coyote, or birds and ants or other insects that would have access to the interior after ripening.

The durability of the cardón is attested to by the mutilation it sometimes receives and survives. In the stand between Bahía de Los Angeles and the old abandoned gold mine smelter site of Las Flores, as well as farther south en route to Bahía de Las Ánimas, may be seen many that have been severely damaged by cattle and perhaps by horses and burros. A number of these plants have had the succulent outside portion eaten completely away down to the woody xylem cylinder (fig. 11.7). The destroyed portion may extend from near the ground upward for as much as three or more feet. Despite this apparently lethal damage, the cardón continues to grow, although probably at a reduced rate, for no one knows how many years.

Fig. 11.6. Typical ripening fruits of the cardón.

Fig. 11.7. Cardón with the succulent outer portion eaten down to the woody vascular cylinder by domestic livestock.

Fig. 11.8. *Datilillo* showing typical branching and terminal flowers.

Fig. 11.9. *Datilillo* flowers as seen between two stems of the same plant.

Yucca valida

Yucca valida, known locally in Baja California as *datilillo,* is only slightly less striking in appearance as a member of the Central Desert than either the boojum or the elephant tree. This tall (20 to 25 feet) yucca resembles the Joshua tree *(Yucca brevifolia)* of Arizona and California both in size and general appearance (fig. 11.8). Both are many-branched, both have the stems clothed with a dense covering of living, or dead, spine-tipped leaves, and both bear clusters of attractive waxy white flowers on the ends of the branches (fig. 11.9).

The principal readily observed difference in the two is in the manner of branching and the consequent general shape of the tree. The *datilillo* is more likely to have two or more main stems, rather than one, originating from near the ground. The branches also tend to be attached at a more acute angle and to grow more nearly vertical than those of the Joshua tree. As a result of these branching habits, the general form of the *datilillo* is less rounded than that of the Joshua tree. It also is usually not as tall, though this can hardly be ascribed to the method of branching.

The name signifies "little date" *(datil+illo)*. From a distance, a grove of *datilillos* looks rather like a grove of date palms. On close examination, the trees bear little resemblance to date palms, but their size, dark green color, and abundant leaves do give them a surprisingly palmlike appearance when seen from afar.

The bases of the woody stems or trunks of the *datilillo* are often as much as a foot thick and may occasionally be up to two feet in diameter. Essentially straight trunks of considerable thickness may be from five to ten feet long and make rather acceptable logs. Because the region produces a dearth of woody material suitable for construction, these trunks, although rather soft and not very durable, are used in building corrals and fences, as roof supports in ramadas and small houses, and in a variety of other ways.

From a botanical and an artistic point of view, however, their real value lies in their beauty and form and the character they give the landscape. The region wouldn't be the same without its *datilillo,* any more than it would be without the boojum or the *torote* or any of its other more striking vegetation forms.

The various plants of the Central Desert all have their own particular preferences as to soil, slope, exposure, temperature, etc. The boojum, for example, does best on a well-drained, medium to coarse-textured soil. The *datilillo,* by contrast, shows a preference for fine-textured soils of a sort often found in wide valleys or gentle slopes leading out from the mountains.

Tillandsia recurvata

This member of the same family as the cultivated pineapple would never be suspected by any but a taxonomist of being even a distant relative of this well-known fruit. In the first place, *Tillandsia recurvata,* known locally in Mexico as *heno pequeño* (little hay) and in the United States as ball moss, produces no pineapples; secondly, it is an epiphyte, clinging by fine aerial roots to trees, shrubs, some cacti, and occasionally to rocky cliffs.

Fig 11.10. *Heno pequeño* perched on its host.

The common American name is rather descriptive, as the plants appear like so many balls of moss clinging to or often almost seeming to smother their host species. On close examination, the Mexican name is also seen to be appropriate, the individual plant clusters resembling small spherical bundles of hay (fig. 11.10).

Heno pequeño thrives in Baja California where moist fog or moisture-bearing winds from the Pacific sweep inland, in some instances as on the road to Bahía de Los Angeles, as much as 30 miles or half-way across the peninsula. I have seen it as far north as Las Palomas and the Desengaño Mine, both about ten miles north of the 29th parallel, but know of no valid reason why it may not occur much further north, since it grows also in southern Arizona, Texas, and Florida.

Several plant species commonly serve as hosts or perches for germination and establishment of *heno pequeño*. A rough bark or cluster of small branches or thorns seem to be, if not requisite, at least highly desir-

Fig. 11.13. Typical thicket of *pitáhaya agria* in the hills east of El Socorro.

may it be more than one of these in just the right combination? We know only that occasional years, as the spring of 1960, and to a lesser extent the spring of 1970, were more than usually favorable for its growth.

Machaerocereus gummosus

No cactus common in central Baja California, with the possible exception of some of the *Opuntias*, presents so formidable an aspect to the cross-country traveler as does *Machaerocereus gummosus* or *pitáhaya agria*. Conversely, only one, *Lemairocereus thurberi* or *pitáhaya dulce,* produces so abundant and edible a fruit. Few plants in the Central Desert are so commonly encountered under as wide a range of habitat conditions as *pitáhaya agria*.

I rather like the description of this cactus as given by the Jesuit historian Clavijero (Standley, 1920–26):

> The branches are straight and narrow like those of the tammia or sweet pitáhaya; but from the trunk they take different directions, without any order or symmetry and, stretching over the ground, they throw out roots and form new plants; interlacing with each other, there result thickets which are unpleasant to look at and impenetrable by animals.

A typical thicket is shown in fig. 11.13. He might have added that, without a machete or axe and considerable labor, these tangled masses are also impenetrable by humans.

The large showy flowers are most abundant in midsummer and ripen to produce the bulk of their fruit during the fall. The strikingly beautiful rose-colored flowers open at night and close, never to reopen, the following morning. The sepals and petals radiate outward for a diameter of about three inches on the end of a tube that may be five to six inches long (fig. 11.14). The fruit that ripens a few months later tends to be globe-shaped and is two to three inches in diameter. These scarlet-colored balls are liberally sprinkled with clusters of spines, but when the fruit is ripe these are easily brushed off. The fleshy interior consists of a juicy mass of purple flesh with a large number of small black seeds (fig. 11.15). The flesh and seeds are eaten together, and have a pleasant, slightly acid taste somewhat like a watermelon to which has been added a touch of lemon.

Considered as the unit that it is, with its truly formibable but still attractive stems and its beautiful flowers and savory fruit, *pitáhaya agria* is a key member of the Central Desert that gives the area much of its character.

Opuntia molesta

Of all the chollas of the Central Desert, none looks more vicious than *Opuntia molesta*. And, should one carelessly acquire too close an acquaintanceship, he is sure that no other *Opuntia* was ever better named. In actual fact, it is probably no more hazardous than some of the other chollas, *O. fulgida* and *O. bigelovii*, for example; it just seems that way because the spines are longer.

Fig. 11.14. Flower of *pitáhaya agria*, one of the Central Desert's most showy flowers.

Fig. 11.15. *Pitáhaya agria* fruit, peeled, quartered, and ready to eat.

Opuntia molesta might be called the long-spined or the golden cholla, though this or any descriptive name is inadequate, since these apply only to appearances, not to the prime spinescent characteristic which is functional, not visual.

If one can overlook the potential discomfort inherent in the plant, it is seen to be extremely attractive, particularly when viewed against the backlight of early morning or late afternoon. The sun shining through the long tawny spines gives the plants a golden luminescence which, paradoxically, both accentuates and softens their hostility (figs. 11.16, 11.17).

The spines, which are the most noticeable thing about the plant, are covered with a papery sheath and may be as much as two inches long. They seem longer than this, particularly after one inadvertently collects a spine-bearing joint and is wondering how best to remove it.

As with most other members of the genus, the terminal joints often fall off and develop roots to establish new plants. These seemingly lie in wait to attack without warning, and one soon learns to walk with extreme caution anywhere in the vicinity of mature plants. The old adage about sleeping dogs applies invariably to joints of *Opuntia molesta*.

The flowers have rather attractive purplish to bronze petals and are from one to two inches in diameter. Although they blossom abundantly in the spring, principally in April and May, the flowers may be overlooked by the nonbotanist partly because they are not as striking as those of many cacti, but primarily because they tend to be overshadowed by the more noticeable spines.

Fig. 11.16. *Opuntia molesta,* a typical mature plant.

Fig. 11.17. Detail of a portion of an *Opuntia molesta* plant, showing its characteristic spininess.

Ambrosia chenopodifolia

This is one of the smaller, although often the most abundant, of the dominant plants in central Baja California. Like the other most common species of the same genus in the area, *A. magdalenae,* this one of the so-called bursages would be more noticed by its absence should it suddenly be removed from the landscape than it is by its presence.

According to Shreve (1951) *A. chenopodifolia* is "the most nearly omnipresent of the shrubby perennials" in the Central Desert, giving "a light-gray tone to the landscape in all but the most rocky situations" (fig. 11.18).

Although it flowers profusely in late winter and spring, the inconspicuous greenish yellow flowers blend in with the gray-green of the leaves and attract little attention. One is more likely to have his attention drawn to the plant by its abundant, spiny seeds which have a tendency to work into open shoe tops and cling to the bottoms of rubber-soled shoes than by any of its visual characteristics.

By its very abundance *Ambrosia chenopodifolia* exerts a considerable influence on the various ecosystems of which it is a part. Its many branches, densely clothed with leaves and growing close to the ground, cast a rather dense shade and provide protection, humus, and a temporarily favorable soil-moisture balance following rains. These characteristics aid in the establishment of and provide a shelter for certain cacti, *Mammillaria* and *Ferocactus* in particular, and for *Idria,* species that typically become established wherever there is some sort of protection from the otherwise harsh environment.

Fortunately for both *Ambrosia chenopodifolia* and *A. magdalenae,* grazing animals, whether rabbits, deer, domestic livestock, or others, find these species unappetizing as forage. Were this not so, extensive portions of the Central Desert would be critically damaged and vegetation composition drastically altered. Not only would the *Ambrosia* be damaged, but those species that require the protection of low-growing shrubs for establishment would be deprived of this essential protection. Other plants that do have some forage value, but that occur too infrequently to attract much grazing pressure, would also be grazed. Extensive grazing, particularly by domestic livestock, would result in trampling and erosion in a region that is currently stable but in general is poorly suited to the kind of disturbance generated by domestic livestock.

Pedilanthus macrocarpus

Shreve (1951) refers to *Pedilanthus macrocarpus (candelilla)* as the only stem succulent, aside from the cacti, in the Sonoran Desert. There are degrees of succulence, and although *Pedilanthus* would appear to be

Fig. 11.18. *Ambrosia chenopodifolia* as the principal understory species in a cardón-cirio "forest."

more succulent than the main stem of *Idria,* both species would seem fundamentally to be stem succulents in that both consist to a large extent of water-storage tissues.

Candelilla belongs to the Euphorbiaceae, and like many members of the family contains a milky sap or latex that exudes at the slightest injury as though it were under great pressure. This "milk" has been indicated by various botanists as reputed to contain rubber or a rubberlike substance (Goldman, 1916; Standley, 1920–26; Dressler, 1957; Shreve and Wiggins, 1964).

The common name *"candelilla"* and the wax-like bloom on the stems has apparently suggested that the stems might have provided wax for making candles. Their use as a source of wax appears doubtful, although the information available that might throw light on this is rather meager. Dressler (1957) suggests *Pedilanthus* as a source of wax, but indicates that earlier accounts may have confused this genus with *Euphorbia antisyphilitica* which is used for its wax.

Only the very young plants are single-stemmed, mature individuals often having so many stems as almost to defy counting (fig. 11.19).

It is often characteristic of the stems that they become fasciated and occasionally assume an extreme cristate form. At times only a few stems of the typically multistemmed plants may be so affected, at other times most of them may be so misshapen. The flowers on such stems seem to develop normally.

Candelilla often germinates and becomes established immediately adjacent to or beneath the protection of other plants, not infrequently the boojum. As *candelilla* is not known to be eaten by any animals, the protection afforded by the nurse plants probably is largely in the nature of a microclimatic tempering of the harsh and arid environment.

The most striking feature of the plant is its flowers. These look like small, bright-red birds, often perched in pairs on the same twig (fig. 11.20). These apparent "flowers" consist of a shoe-shaped, hoodlike involucre containing the true flowers. (The highly descriptive name, from the Greek, indicates a sandal [*pedil*] and a kind of bird [*anthos*]). There are several male flowers within each involucre, each consisting of a single

Fig. 11.19. *Candelilla* in full bloom, overtopping its original nurse plant, *Lophocereus schottii.*

Fig. 11.20.
Candelilla "flower."

Fig. 11.21.
Candelilla fruits.

stamen. In addition, each involucre contains a single pistillate flower which may or may not have a perianth of three minute scales. The cluster of stamens protrudes from the involucre somewhat like a bird's topknot (or, less esthetically, like a chicken's neck from which the head has just been wrung), while the developing ovary droops below, bearing a rather strong resemblance to the conical beak of some exotic bird. The involucre itself is strongly suggestive of a red-bodied bird from which all the feathers have been plucked. Surely, this is one of the most unbelievable flowers in an unbelievable land.

Later, the developing fruits, although not as bizarre-appearing as the flowers, have their own claim to uniqueness, as indicated by fig. 11.21.

Appendixes

APPENDIX A

Scientific and Common Names of Plants Referred to in the Text

TABLE A-1
Plants referred to in text

SCIENTIFIC NAME	COMMON NAME(S)
Abies concolor	white fir
Acacia greggii	catclaw, *uña de gato*
Acalypha californica	
Adenostoma fasciculatum	chamiso
Aesculus parryi	buckeye
Agave deserti	desert mescal
Agave shawii	Shaw's mescal
Alvordia fruticosa	
Ambrosia bryantii	star bursage
Ambrosia camphorata	camphor bursage
Ambrosia chenopodifolia	goosefoot bursage
Ambrosia deltoidea	triangle bursage
Ambrosia dumosa	white bursage
Ambrosia magdalenae	Magdalen bursage
Anaptychia leucomelaena	
Antigonon leptopus	queen's wreath
Arctostaphylos sp.	manzanita
Aristida sp.	three-awn
Artemisia californica	California sagebrush
Asclepias sp.	milkweed
Atamisquea emarginata	
Atriplex barclayana	saltbush
Atriplex julacea	saltbush
Atriplex polycarpa	desert saltbush
Beloperone californica	
Bronnia sp.	
Bursera hindsiana	*copalquín*
Bursera microphylla	*copalquín, copal*
Calliandra californica	*huajillo,* false mesquite, bastard mesquite
Caloplaca aurantiaca	lichen

SCIENTIFIC NAME	COMMON NAME(S)
Caloplaca holocarpa	lichen
Cardiospermum corindum	bladderpod
Carnegiea gigantea	sahuaro
Cassia covesii	senna
Ceanothus sp.	buckbrush
Cercidium microphyllum	foothill paloverde
Cercidium peninsulare	paloverde, *palo de pua*
Cercocarpus betuloides	mountain mahogany
Cercocarpus minutiflorus	mountain mahogany
Coldenia canescens	
Condalia spathulata	
Cuscuta veatchii	dodder
Dalea emoryi	
Dideria sp.	
Ditaxis lanceolata	
Dudleya acuminata	live-forever
Echinocereus sp.	hedgehog cactus
Encelia californica	California brittlebush
Encelia californica v. *asperifolia*	
Encelia farinosa	brittlebush
Ephedra spp.	Mormon tea
Eriogonum fasciculatum	shrubby buckwheat
Eriogonum inflatum v. *deflatum*	wild buckwheat
Erodium cicutarium	filaree, alfilaria, stork's bill
Errazurizia megacarpa	
Erythea armata	blue palm
Eucalyptus sp.	
Euphorbia antisyphilitica	*candelilla*
Euphorbia misera	
Euphorbia tomentulosa	
Eurotia lanata	winterfat, whitesage
Fagonia californica	
Ferocactus acanthodes	barrel cactus, *bisnaga, visnaga*
Fouquieria campanulata	
Fouquieria diguetii	ocotillo
Fouquieria fasciculata	ocotillo
Fouquieria purpusii	
Fouquieria shrevei	
Fouquieria splendens	ocotillo

SCIENTIFIC NAME	COMMON NAME(S)
Frankenia palmeri	
Fraxinus velutina	velvet ash, Arizona ash, *fresno*
Galium sp.	bedstraw
Gutierrezia bracteata	snakeweed
Hibiscus sp.	rose-mallow, hibiscus
Hilaria belangeri	curly mesquite
Hilaria mutica	tobosa
Hilaria rigida	giant tobosa
Hofmeisteria laphamioides	
Hosackia glabra v. *brevialata*	smooth deervetch
Hyptis spp.	
Idria columnaris	*cirio,* boojum tree, *idria, milapa*
Jatropha cinerea	*zapo*
Jatropha cuneata	*sangre de drago, torote prieto*
Juniperus californica	California juniper
Krameria grayi	white ratany, range ratany
Larrea tridentata	creosotebush, *gobernadora*
Lecanora sp.	lichen
Lemairocereus thurberi	organpipe cactus, *pitáhaya dulce*
Libocedrus decurrens	incense cedar
Lophocereus schottii	old man cactus, *senito*
Lycium californicum	*tomatillo*
Lyrocarpa coulteri	wild mustard
Lysiloma candida	*palo blanco*
Lysiloma microphylla	*palo blanco*
Machaerocereus gummosus	*pitáhaya agria*
Mammillaria sp.	fishhook cactus
Mirabilis bigelovii	four-o'clock
Mirabilis bigelovii v. *aspera*	four-o'clock
Muhlenbergia sp.	muhly
Myrtilocactus cochal	Santa Maria cactus
Olneya tesota	ironwood, *palo fierro*
Opuntia arbuscula	pencil cholla
Opuntia bigelovii	teddybear cholla
Opuntia cholla	cholla
Opuntia engelmannii	prickly pear
Opuntia fulgida	jumping cholla
Opuntia leptocaulis	Christmas cactus
Opuntia molesta	devil's cholla
Opuntia ramosissima	diamond cholla

SCIENTIFIC NAME	COMMON NAME(S)
Opuntia spinosior	staghorn cholla
Pachycereus pecten-aboriginum	*cardón hecho, hecho*
Pachycereus pringlei	cardón
Pachycormus discolor	*copalquín, torote blanco,* elephant tree
Pachypodium sp.	
Parkinsonia aculeata	Mexican paloverde
Pedilanthus macrocarpa	*candelilla*
Phoradendron sp.	mistletoe
Phrygilanthus sp.	mistletoe
Physicia aipolia	lichen
Pinus cembroides	pinyon or nut pine
Pinus contorta	lodgepole pine
Pinus edulis	pinyon or nut pine
Pinus lambertiana	sugar pine, yellow pine
Pinus monophylla	pinyon or nut pine
Pinus ponderosa v. *jeffreyi*	Jeffrey pine, yellow pine
Pinus quadrifolia	pinyon or nut pine
Platanus racemosa	California sycamore, planetree
Polygala desertorum	
Populus fremontii	*álamo,* Fremont cottonwood
Populus tremuloides	quaking aspen
Porophyllum gracile	stinkweed, *hierba de venado*
Prosopis juliflora v. *torreyana*	mesquite
Pseudotsuga taxifolia	Douglasfir
Psilostrophe cooperi	paperflower
Quercus agrifolia	coast liveoak
Quercus chrysolepis	canyon oak
Quercus palmeri	Palmer's oak
Ramalina ceruchis	lichen
Ramalina reticulata	beardmoss
Ramalina testudinaria	lichen
Rosa minutifolia	wild rose
Salsola kali	tumbleweed, Russian thistle
Sequoia sp.	redwood
Simmondsia chinensis	coffeeberry, *jojoba*
Solanum hindsianum	
Sphaeralcea sp.	sore-eyes
Stephanomeria pauciflora	
Tecoma stans	trumpet flower, *palo de arco*
Tillandsia recurvata	*heno pequeño,* ball moss

SCIENTIFIC NAME	COMMON NAME(S)
Tribulus terrestris	puncture weed, bullhead, caltrop
Trixis californica	
Viguiera deltoidea	
Viguiera microphylla	
Viguiera purisimae	
Viguiera tomentosa	
Viscainoa geniculata	
Washingtonia robusta	fan palm
Xanthoria elegans	
Xanthoria polycarpa	
Xylonagra arborea v. *wigginsii*	
Yucca brevifolia	Joshua tree
Yucca schidigera	yucca, soapweed, *datil,* Spanish bayonet
Yucca valida	*datilillo*
Yucca whipplei v. *eremica*	*datil*
Zinnia pumila	desert zinnia

APPENDIX B

Insects Collected on *Idria* Blossoms, 1967–70

TABLE B-1
Insects on *Idria* blossoms

Classification	*Locality* Son.	B.C.	*Year* '67	'68	'69	'70
Order Hymenoptera						
F.* Andrenidae						
Perdita michelbacheri Timb.		X			16***	
F. Apidae						
SF.** Anthophorinae						
Anthophora c. californica Cr.		X			3	
Melissodes tessellata LaB.		X			16	
Triepeolus verbesinae (Ckll.)		X		2		
SF. Alpinae						
Apis mellifera L.	X	X	1	1	1	1
Centris rhodopus Ckll.	X					1
SF. Xylocopinae						
Ceratina spp.	X					20
Xylocopa californica arizonensis Cr.		X			2	
		X	[illegible]	1		
		X			1	
	X		[illegible]	[illegible]		
F. Braconidae	X					1
F. Halictidae						
Agapostemon texanus C.		X			15	
Dialictus spp.	X		2			
	X			4		
	X					7
		X		4		
		X		1		
F. Formicidae		X		66		
		X			6	
	X					2
F. Leucospidae	X					1

*Family
**Subfamily
***Numeral indicates number of collections

TABLE B-1 (cont'd)
Insects on *Idria* blossoms

Classification	Locality: Son.	Locality: B.C.	Year: '67	Year: '68	Year: '69	Year: '70
Order Hymenoptera (cont'd)						
F. Megachilidae						
Ashmeadiella sp.	X					2
Chalicodoma (Chelostomoides) browni Mitch.		X			3	
Chalicodoma (Chelostomoides) ignacensis Mitch.	X					1
Chalicodoma (Chelostomoides) lobatifrons Ckll.		X			4	
	X					4
Chalicodoma (Chelostomoides) occidentalis Fox ?	X					1
Lithurgus (Lithurgopsis) echinocacti Ckll.		X			5	
		X			5	
Megachile (Litomegachile) lippiae Ckll.		X			2	
	X					6
Megachile (Pseudocentron) sidalceae Ckll.	X					1
Megachile (Litomegachile) texana Cress.	X					1
Stelis sp.	X					1
F. Sphecidae		X			2	
SF. Bemicinae		X			2	
F. Vespidae		X			2	
SF. Eumeninae	X					4
Order Diptera						
F. Asilidae		X			1	
F. Bombyliidae	X					3
F. Syrphidae		X			3	
Nausigaster sp.	X					1
Misc. Superfam. Calyptratae	X					11

TABLE B-1 (cont'd)
Insects on *Idria* blossoms

Classification	*Locality*		*Year*			
	Son.	*B.C.*	*'67*	*'68*	*'69*	*'70*
Order Lepidoptera						
F. Hesperiidae						
Erynnis sp.	X		5			
	X					6
		X			1	
F. Lycaenidae	X		8			
		X		5		
		X			1	
	X					10
F. Pieridae	X					2
Misc. Moths		X			3	
	X					2
Order Coleoptera						
F. Anobiidae		X			2	
F. Anthicidae	X					1
F. Chrysomelidae						
SF. Cryptocephalinae		X			3	
F. Cleridae		X			1	
	X					2
F. Malachiidae		X			2	
	X					5
F. Melyridae						
SF. Dasytinae		X		ca. 150		
		X			ca. 275	
F. Mordellidae		X			2	
Order Hemiptera						
F. Pentatomidae	X				1	
F. Tingidae	X					1
Misc. Arachnida (spiders, etc.)		X			2	
	X					1

APPENDIX C

Plant Composition Under Varying Environmental Conditions

TABLE C-1

Plant composition on north exposures at Punta Cirio

Taxa	Frequence			
	Ave. per 100 ft. by clusters			
	A	*B*	*C*	*Mean*
Ambrosia deltoidea	0	.3	0	.1
Ambrosia dumosa	1.9	2.5	1.5	2.0
Beloperone californica	0	0	.1	.0
Bursera microphylla	.9	.5	.2	.5
Cercidium microphyllum	.1	.5	0	.2
Dalea sp.	0	.4	0	.1
Ditaxis lanceolata	.1	.7	.1	.3
Encelia farinosa	2.8	2.2	1.2	2.1
Eriogonum fasciculatum	0	.4	0	.1
Euphorbia misera	.3	.6	0	.3
Fagonia californica	0	4.8	.8	1.9
Fouquieria splendens	.5	.6	.2	.4
Hibiscus sp.	.1	.3	.1	.2
Hofmeisteria laphamioides	.3	0	.1	.1
Hyptis sp.	0	0	.1	.0
Idria columnaris	.1	.6	.6	.4
Jatropha cuneata	1.4	1.6	1.6	1.5
Larrea tridentata	.1	.4	1.0	.5
Lycium californicum	.5	.2	.4	.4
Lyrocarpa coulteri	0	.1	0	.0
Olneya tesota	0	.2	0	.1
Opuntia bigelovii	.1	.1	0	.1
Porophyllum gracile	0	.2	0	.1
Simmondsia chinensis	.9	0	.2	.4
Solanum hindsianum	1.5	.8	.4	.9
Sphaeralcea sp.	.3	2.5	.7	1.2
Stephanomeria pauciflora	0	.4	0	.1
Total	11.9	20.9	15.5	14.0
Number of taxa	17	23	15	18.3
Less trace taxa (.1)	11	21	12	

TABLE C-2

Plant composition on a south exposure at Punta Cirio

Taxa	Frequence
	Ave. per 100 ft.
Ambrosia dumosa	.7
Bursera hindsiana	.1
Bursera microphylla	1.3
Cercidium microphyllum	.4
Dalea sp.	.2
Ditaxis lanceolata	.2
Encelia farinosa	4.5
Euphorbia misera	.2
Fagonia californica	.5
Fouquieria splendens	.7
Hibiscus sp.	.6
Jatropha cuneata	4.0
Lophocereus schottii	.1
Olneya tesota	.2
Opuntia bigelovii	.7
Sphaeralcea sp.	.1
Total	14.5
Number of taxa	16
Less trace taxa (.1)	13

TABLE C-3

Plant composition on northwest exposures at Punta Cuevas

Taxa	Frequence			
	Ave. per 100 ft. by clusters			
	A	*B*	*C*	*Mean*
Ambrosia deltoidea	0	.3	1.0	.1
Ambrosia dumosa	.8	2.5	2.3	1.9
Bursera microphylla	1.5	.5	.9	.9
Cercidium microphyllum	.6	.5	.3	.5
Dalea sp.	0	.4	0	.1
Ditaxis lanceolata	.1	.7	.5	.4
Encelia farinosa	.9	2.2	1.1	1.4
Eriogonum fasciculatum	0	.4	.1	.2
Euphorbia misera	.4	.6	.5	.5
Fagonia californica	0	4.8	0	1.6
Ferocactus acanthodes	0	0	.07	.0
Fouquieria splendens	.3	.6	.5	.5
Hibiscus sp.	0	.3	.5	.3
Idria columnaris	.5	.6	.4	.5
Jatropha cuneata	2.2	1.6	3.0	2.3
Krameria grayi	0	0	.1	.0
Larrea tridentata	0	.4	.1	.2
Lophocereus schottii	.1	0	.07	.1
Lycium californicum	.2	.2	.07	.2
Lyrocarpa coulteri	0	.1	0	.0
Olneya tesota	0	.2	.07	.1
Opuntia bigelovii	0	.1	0	.0
Porophyllum gracile	0	.2	0	.1
Simmondsia chinensis	.7	0	0	.2
Solanum hindsianum	3.1	.8	0	1.3
Sphaeralcea sp.	.3	2.5	.07	1.0
Stephanomeria pauciflora	0	.4	0	.1
Trixis californica	.2	0	0	.1
Total	11.9	20.9	11.65	14.6
Number of taxa	15	23	19	28
Less trace taxa (.1)	13	21	11	

TABLE C-4

Plant composition on a south exposure at Punta Cuevas

Taxa	Frequence		
	Ave. per 100 ft. by clusters		
	A	*B*	*Mean*
Bursera microphylla	1.4	1.9	1.7
Cercidium microphyllum	1.2	.4	.8
Dalea sp.	0	.8	.4
Ditaxis lanceolata	.5	0	.3
Encelia farinosa	.7	.7	.7
Eriogonum fasciculatum	.2	4.6	2.4
Fagonia californica	2.9	2.9	2.9
Fouquieria splendens	.2	.1	.2
Hibiscus sp.	0	.1	.1
Jatropha cuneata	2.8	3.2	3.0
Lophocereus schottii	0	.1	.1
Olneya tesota	.3	.3	.3
Opuntia bigelovii	.9	.4	.7
Pachycereus pringlei	0	.1	.1
Porophyllum gracile	0	.5	.3
Simmondsia chinensis	.3	.3	.3
Solanum hindsianum	0	1	.1
Sphaeralcea sp.	.9	.7	.8
Trixis californica	.1	0	.1
Total	12.4	17.2	15.3
Number of taxa	13	17	19
Less trace taxa (.1)	12	11	

TABLE C-5

Plant composition on coarse sandy loam at Desengaño Triangle, Gold Mine Camp, and Camp Víbora

Taxa	*Frequence*										
	Ave. per 100 ft. by clusters										
	A	*B*	*C*	*D*	*E*	*F*	*G*	*H*	*I*	*J*	*Mean*
Acalypha californica	0	0	0	0	.4	.2	0	0	0	0	.06
Agave deserti	0	0	.1	0	0	0	.9	.7	5.2	5.2	1.21
Agave shawii	.2	0	.2	.5	0	0	1.9	.8	.7	1.6	.59
Ambrosia chenopodifolia	0	0	2.0	2.8	0	0	1.6	3.1	2.4	.1	1.20
Ambrosia dumosa	.5	2.7	0	0	.1	0	.2	0	0	.3	.38
Ambrosia magdalenae	2.1	.9	.1	.9	.1	0	3.6	4.6	2.1	1.8	1.62
Beloperone californica	0	0	0	.2	.4	.3	0	0	.1	0	.10
Bursera hindsiana	0	0	0	0	.4	.3	0	0	0	0	.07
Encelia californica v. *asperifolia*	.1	.6	.1	.6	.2	.7	0	.4	.2	.2	.31
Encelia farinosa	0	0	0	0	0	0	0	0	.6	.5	.11
Eriogonum fasciculatum	.2	0	.1	.4	0	0	.3	.4	.1	0	.15
Hosackia glabra v. *brevialata*	0	0	0	0	0	8.1	1.1	1.8	0	0	1.10
Idria columnaris	.3	.1	.4	.3	.6	.1	.1	0	.2	.3	.24
Jatropha cinerea	0	0	0	0	.1	.8	0	0	0	0	.09
Krameria grayi	0	0	0	0	0	0	.5	.7	.6	.3	.21

Larrea tridentata	.5	1.1	.4	.7	.1	0	.5	.2	.4	1.0	.49
Lophocereus schottii	.3	.2	[illegible]	.4	0	0	.1	.1	.1	.1	.14
Lycium spp.	.7	1.2	3.9	1.2	0	0	0	0	0	.3	.73
Machaerocereus gummosus	0	0	0	.2	0	0	.5	0	.1	.2	.10
Mirabilis bigelovii	.6	.6	0	0	0	.1	.3	.3	0	.1	.20
Opuntia cholla	.1	[illegible]	0	0	0	.1	1.1	.4	.8	.7	.33
Opuntia molesta	0	0	0	0	.2	.8	0	.2	.1	.4	.17
Opuntia spp.	0	0	0	.2	.9	0	0	0	0	.1	.12
Pachycereus pringlei	.2	[illegible]	.1	0	0	0	0	0	0	.1	.06
Pedilanthus macrocarpus	1.1	[illegible]	.1	0	0	.6	.7	.9	.2	.4	.48
Prosopis juliflora v. *torreyana*	.2	0	.3	.1	.1	0	.1	.2	0	.4	.14
Simmondsia chinensis	.4	.2	.2	0	.2	0	.1	.1	.3	.2	.17
Viscainoa geniculata	.4	.3	0	.2	.3	.9	0	0	0	0	.21
Yucca valida	.3	.1	.2	0	0	0	0	0	.3	.2	.11
Totals	8.2	9.1	8.5	8.7	4.1	13.0	13.6	14.9	14.5	14.5	10.90
Number of taxa	17	14	15	14	14	12	17	16	18	22	29
Less trace taxa (.1)	15	11	8	13	9	9	13	14	13	17	

TABLE C-6

Plant composition on a shale-derived soil near Gold Mine Camp

Taxa	Frequence		
	Ave. per 100 ft. by clusters		
	A	*B*	*Mean*
Agave deserti	.5	12.9	6.70
Ambrosia dumosa	3.7	2.3	3.00
Ambrosia magdalenae	.1	0	.05
Bursera microphylla	.1	0	.05
Cassia covesii	0	.1	.05
Dalea emoryi	.5	0	.25
Ditaxis sp.	0	.1	.05
Encelia californica	0	1.0	.50
Encelia farinosa	0	.9	.45
Eriogonum fasciculatum	0	.2	.10
Euphorbia tomentulosa	0	.1	.05
Ferocactus acanthodes	.1	0	.05
Fouquieria splendens	.8	.2	.50
Hosackia glabra v. *brevialata*	0	.1	.05
Idria columnaris	.6	.2	.40
Krameria grayi	1.2	.3	.75
Larrea tridentata	1.4	.4	.90
Lophocereus schottii	0	.1	.05
Lyrocarpa coulteri	.1	.1	.10
Machaerocereus gummosus	.3	0	.15
Mirabilis bigelovii	.1	.2	.15
Muhlenbergia sp.	.2	0	.10
Opuntia cholla	.2	.2	.20
Opuntia molesta	.1	0	.05
Pachycereus pringlei	.2	0	.10
Pedilanthus macrocarpus	1.0	0	.50
Simmondsia chinensis	0	.2	.10
Total	11.2	19.6	15.40
Number of taxa	18	18	18
Less trace taxa (.1)	12	12	

TABLE C-7

Plant composition on Cerrito Blanco volcanic ash

Taxa	Frequence				
	Ave. per 100 ft. by clusters				
	A	*B*	*C*	*D*	*Mean*
Agave deserti	.7	3.0	3.2	2.7	2.40
Agave shawii	0	0	0	1.0	.25
Ambrosia chenopodifolia	5.5	4.8	3.0	3.3	4.15
Asclepias sp.	0	.1	.1	0	.05
Calliandra californica	0	.2	.3	.1	.15
Coldenia canescens	0	.1	.1	0	.05
Encelia californica	.2	.2	.1	.1	.15
Eriogonum fasciculatum	1.2	1.7	0	1.5	1.10
Eriogonum sp.	0	0	.3	0	.08
Eurotia lanata	.8	.3	0	.1	.30
Fouquieria splendens	0	0	.4	.4	.20
Idria columnaris	.1	0	.1	.1	.08
Krameria grayi	1.1	1.2	.1	.9	.83
Larrea tridentata	1.7	.4	.5	.3	.73
Polygala desertorum	0	0	0	.3	.08
Porophyllum gracile	.1	.1	0	.1	.08
Simmondsia chinensis	.1	.2	.4	.1	.20
Zinnia pumila	.2	.3	.1	0	.15
Total	11.8	12.6	8.7	11.0	11.00
Number of taxa	11	12	12	14	18
Less trace taxa (.1)	8	10	7	8	

TABLE C-8

Plant composition on a camphorata clay soil near El Arenoso

Taxa	Frequence			
	Ave. per 100 ft. by clusters			
	A	*B*	*C*	*Mean*
Agave deserti	2.0	2.6	3.1	2.57
Agave shawii	3.6	2.6	.9	2.37
Ambrosia camphorata	4.8	2.5	4.0	3.77
Ambrosia chenopodifolia	.7	1.4	2.5	1.53
Echinocereus sp.	.1	.2	0	.10
Encelia californica	1.9	1.6	1.3	1.60
Eriogonum fasciculatum	2.7	2.3	.2	1.73
Eriogonum sp.	.6	0	0	.20
Euphorbia misera	.5	.2	0	.23
Euphorbia tomentulosa	.4	.5	.1	.33
Ferocactus acanthodes	.3	0	0	.10
Hosackia sp.	.6	.3	.1	.33
Hyptis sp.	.7	0	0	.23
Idria columnaris	.3	.4	0	.23
Lycium californicum	0	.3	.5	.27
Machaerocereus gummosus	0	.3	.3	.20
Mammillaria sp.	.2	0	.1	.10
Opuntia cholla	.3	.2	.5	.33
Opuntia engelmannii	.2	.1	.5	.27
Opuntia molesta	.3	.6	.7	.53
Opuntia spinosior	.2	.3	.3	.27
Prosopis juliflora v. *torreyana*	.2	.1	0	.10
Simmondsia chinensis	.2	.6	.1	.30
Solanum hindsianum	.1	.6	.1	.27
Viguiera deltoidea	.5	.2	.2	.30
Total	21.4	17.9	15.5	18.27
Number of taxa	23	21	18	
Less trace taxt (.1)	21	19	13	

TABLE C-9

Plant composition on San Fernando limestone and rhyolite soils

Taxa	Frequence	
	Ave. per 100 ft. by clusters	
	A (limestone)	*B (rhyolite)*
Agave deserti	.3	.6
Ambrosia chenopodifolia	5.7	5.8
Ambrosia magdalenae	0	4.1
Echinocereus sp.	0	.2
Encelia californica	4.9	2.5
Eriogonum fasciculatum	2.0	1.7
Fagonia californica	.2	0
Ferocactus acanthodes	.1	.2
Hyptis sp.	0	.1
Idria columnaris	.4	0
Krameria grayi	0	.2
Larrea tridentata	.4	0
Lophocereus schottii	0	.2
Lycium sp.	.3	.3
Mirabilis bigelovii	.2	0
Opuntia spp.	.2	0
Porophyllum gracile	.2	.1
Simmondsia chinensis	.1	0
Solanum hindsianum	.3	.1
Total	15.3	16.1
Number of taxa	14	13
Less trace taxa (.1)	11	10

TABLE C-10

Plant composition on a granitic soil near El Ciprés

Taxa	Frequence
	Ave. per 100 ft.
Agave deserti	5.7
Agave shawii	.4
Ambrosia chenopodifolia	2.7
Ambrosia magdalenae	2.8
Dudleya sp.	.1
Eriogonum fasciculatum	6.9
Ferocactus acanthodes	.1
Fouquieria splendens	.1
Hosackia sp.	.1
Idria columnaris	.3
Rosa minutifolia	.1
Total	20.0
Number of taxa	12
Less trace taxa (.1)	7

TABLE C-11

Plant composition on a granitic soil near Agua Dulce

Taxa	Frequence
	Ave. per 100 ft.
Agave deserti	4.3
Ambrosia dumosa	6.1
Encelia californica	1.4
Ephedra sp.	.1
Euphorbia tomentulosa	.1
Eurotia lanata	.4
Fouquieria splendens	.5
Gutierrezia bracteata	.5
Krameria grayi	.8
Larrea tridentata	1.1
Opuntia arbuscula	.4
Psilostrophe cooperi	.7
Simmondsia chinensis	.4
Total	16.8
Number of taxa	13
Less trace taxa (.1)	11

TABLE C-12

Plant composition — Las Arrastras clay

Taxa	Frequence		
	Ave. per 100 ft. by clusters		
	A	*B*	*Mean*
Agave deserti	0	.2	.1
Atriplex barclayana	21.6	15.2	18.4
Errazurizia megacarpa	0	.3	.15
Fouquieria splendens	0	.1	.05
Idria columnaris	0	.1	.05
Jatropha cuneata	.6	.4	.5
Larrea tridentata	.1	.2	.15
Opuntia ramosissima	0	.3	.15
Pachycormus discolor	.1	.3	.2
Prosopis juliflora v. (?)	.1	0	.05
Total	22.5	17.1	19.8
Number of taxa	5	9	
Less trace taxa (.1)	2	7	

TABLE C-13

Plant composition — basaltic plains, Rosarito to San Borja

Taxa	Frequence		
	Ave. per 100 ft. by clusters		
	A	*B*	*Mean*
Agave shawii	.7	.3	.50
Ambrosia chenopodifolia	.3	.8	.55
Atriplex barclayana	0	1.0	.50
Atriplex julacea	2.5	1.8	2.15
Atriplex polycarpa	2.4	0	1.20
Encelia californica	0	.1	.05
Eriogonum inflatum v. *deflatum*	.1	0	.05
Euphorbia misera	.6	0	.30
Fagonia californica	.2	0	.10
Ferocactus acanthodes	.1	0	.05
Fouquieria diguetii	0	.3	.15
Idria columnaris	.2	.3	.25
Jatropha cinerea	.1	0	.05
Larrea tridentata	0	.1	.05
Lophocereus schottii	0	.1	.05
Lycium californicum	0	.5	.25
Machaerocereus gummosus	.4	.5	.45
Opuntia cholla	.3	.2	.25
Opuntia molesta	0	.2	.10
Opuntia ramosissima	.2	0	.10
Opuntia spinosior	0	.2	.10
Pachycereus pringlei	0	.1	.05
Pachycormus discolor	.5	.4	.45
Sphaeralcea sp.	0	.1	.05
Viguiera microphylla	.3	0	.15
Total	8.9	7.0	7.95
Number of taxa	15	17	
Less trace taxa (.1)	12	12	

TABLE C-14

Plant composition — basalt clay loam, Arroyo del Rosario

Taxa	Frequence
	Ave. per 100 ft.
Ambrosia chenopodifolia	9.3
Atriplex julacea	.1
Atriplex polycarpa	.1
Dudleya sp.	.1
Euphorbia misera	1.1
Idria columnaris	.2
Lycium sp.	2.0
Machaerocereus gummosus	1.1
Opuntia cholla	1.3
Opuntia sp.	.6
Total	15.9
Number of taxa	10
Less trace taxa (.1)	7

TABLE C-15

Plant composition — Cajiloa coastal plain

Taxa	Frequence
	Ave. per 100 ft.
Ambrosia bryantii	5.1
Ambrosia chenopodifolia	2.0
Atriplex julacea	.9
Cardiospermum corindum	.2
Encelia farinosa	1.2
Euphorbia misera	1.3
Ferocactus acanthodes	.1
Fouquieria splendens	.1
Idria columnaris	.3
Lycium spp.	1.2
Machaerocereus gummosus	2.0
Mirabilis bigelovii v. *aspera*	.1
Opuntia cholla	.3
Pachycereus pringlei	.3
Prosopis juliflora v. (?)	.2
Yucca whipplei v. *eremica*	1.2
Total	16.5
Number of taxa	16
Less trace taxa (.1)	13

TABLE C-16

Plant composition at Pacific coastal areas from Las Palomas to Punta Falsa

Taxa	Frequence				
	Ave. per 100 ft. by clusters				
	A	*B*	*C*	*D*	*Mean*
Aesculus parryi	.1	0	0	0	.02
Agave shawii	1.6	.8	.8	0	.80
Ambrosia chenopodifolia	1.7	6.7	.1	3.0	2.87
Ambrosia magdalenae	.6	0	0	0	.15
Atriplex julacea	0	0	4.4	0	1.10
Atriplex spp.	.4	0	0	0	.10
Bursera microphylla	.1	.2	0	0	.07
Cardiospermum corindum	0	.6	0	0	.15
Dudleya acuminata	0	0	0	24.0	3.50
Encelia californica	1.3	.1	0	0	.35
Eriogonum fasciculatum	.1	8.4	0	0	2.12
Euphorbia misera	1.3	1.5	.9	5.3	2.25
Frankenia palmeri	1.9	0	7.4	17.0	6.57
Idria columnaris	.1	1.3	0	2.3	.92
Lycium spp.	.7	1.3	.2	.3	.62
Machaerocereus gummosus	0	.1	0	0	.13
Mammillaria spp.	0	0	0	.3	.07
Myrtilocactus cochal	.1	0	0	0	.02
Opuntia leptocaulis	.7	.9	.3	0	.42
Porophyllum gracile	.3	0	0	0	.07
Solanum hindsianum	.2	0	0	0	.05
Sphaeralcea sp.	0	.2	0	0	.05
Trixis californica	0	.1	0	0	.02
Unknown	0	.4	.1	0	.12
Viguiera purisimae	0	.7	0	0	.17
Xylonagra arborea v. *wigginsii*	0	.5	0	4.7	1.30
Total	11.2	23.8	14.2	46.9	24.02
Number of taxa	16	16	8	8	26
Less trace taxa (.1)	11	13	6	8	

TABLE C-17

Taxa occurrence by transect cluster *

Taxa	*Sonora* 1	2	3	4	*Cluster Frequency*	*Baja California* 5	6	7	8	9	10	11	12	13	14	15	16	*Cluster Frequency*	*Total Cluster Frequency*
Acalypha californica						X												1	1
Aesculus parryi																	X	1	1
Agave deserti						X	X	X	X	X	X	X	X					8	8
Agave shawii						X		X	X		X			X			X	6	6
Ambrosia bryantii																X		1	1
Ambrosia camphorata									X									1	1
Ambrosia chenopodifolia						X		X	X	X	X			X	X	X	X	9	9
Ambrosia deltoidea	X		X		2														2
Ambrosia dumosa	X	X	X		3	X	X					X						3	6
Ambrosia magdalenae						X	X			X	X						X	5	5
Asclepias sp.								X										1	1
Atriplex barclayana													X	X				2	2
Atriplex julacea														X	X	X	X	4	4
Atriplex polycarpa														X	X			2	2
Atriplex sp.																	X	1	1
Beloperone californica	X				1	X												1	2
Bursera hindsiana		X			1	X												1	2
Bursera microphylla	X	X	X	X	4												X	1	5
Calliandra californica								X										1	1
Cardiospermum corindum																X	X	2	2
Cercidium microphyllum	X	X	X	X	4														4
Coldenia canescens								X										1	1
Dalea emoryi	X	X	X	X	4														4
Dalea sp.							X											1	1
Ditaxis lanceolata	X	X	X	X	4														4
Ditaxis sp.							X											1	1
Dudleya acuminata																	X	1	1
Dudleya spp.											X				X			2	2

*Column numbers 1 through 16 correspond to table numbers C-1 through C-16.

(cont'd)

TABLE C-17 (cont'd)

Taxa occurrence by transect cluster *

Taxa	*Sonora*				*Cluster Frequency*	*Baja California*												*Cluster Frequency*	*Total Cluster Frequency*
	1	2	3	4		5	6	7	8	9	10	11	12	13	14	15	16		
Echinocereus sp.									X	X								2	2
Encelia californica							X	X	X	X				X			X	6	6
Encelia californica v. *asperifolia*						X												1	1
Encelia farinosa	X	X	X	X	4	X	X									X		3	7
Ephedra sp.												X						1	1
Eriogonum fasciculatum	X		X	X	3	X	X	X	X	X	X						X	7	10
Eriogonum inflatum v. *deflatum*														X				1	1
Eriogonum sp.								X	X									2	2
Errazurizia megacarpa													X					1	1
Euphorbia misera	X	X	X		3				X					X	X	X	X	5	8
Euphorbia tomentulosa							X		X			X						3	3
Eurotia lanata								X				X						2	2
Fagonia californica	X	X	X	X	4					X				X				2	6
Ferocactus acanthodes			X		1		X		X	X	X			X		X		6	7
Fouquieria diguetii														X				1	1
Fouquieria splendens	X	X	X	X	4		X	X			X	X	X			X		6	10
Frankenia palmeri																	X	1	1
Gutierrezia bracteata												X						1	1
Hibiscus sp.	X	X	X	X	4														4
Hofmeisteria laphamioides	X				1														1
Hosackia glabra v. *brevialata*						X	X											2	2
Hosackia sp.									X		X							2	2
Hyptis sp.	X				1				X	X								2	3
Idria columnaris	X		X		2	X	X	X	X	X	X		X	X	X	X	X	10	12
Jatropha cinerea						X								X				2	2
Jatropha cuneata	X	X	X	X	4								X					1	5
Krameria grayi			X		1	X	X	X		X		X						5	6

Larrea tridentata	X		X		2	X	X	X		X		X	X	X				7	9
Lophocereus schottii		X	X	X	3	X	X			X				X				4	7
Lycium californicum	X		X		2				X					X				2	4
Lycium spp.						X				X					X	X	X	5	5
Lyrocarpa coulteri	X		X		2		X											1	3
Machaerocereus gummosus						X	X		X					X	X	X	X	7	7
Mammillaria sp.									X								X	2	2
Mirabilis bigelovii						X	X			X								3	3
Mirabilis bigelovii v. *aspera*																X		1	1
Muhlenbergia sp.							X											1	1
Myrtillocactus cochal																	X	1	1
Olneya tesota	X	X	X	X	4														4
Opuntia arbuscula												X						1	1
Opuntia bigelovii	X	X	X	X	4														4
Opuntia cholla						X	X		X					X	X	X		6	6
Opuntia engelmannii									X									1	1
Opuntia leptocaulis																	X	1	1
Opuntia molesta						X	X		X					X				4	4
Opuntia ramosissima													X	X				2	2
Opuntia spinosior						X				X					X			3	3
Opuntia spp.									X					X				2	2
Pachycereus pringlei				X	1	X	X							X		X		4	5
Pachycormus discolor													X	X				2	2
Pedilanthus macrocarpus						X	X											2	2
Polygala desertorum								X										1	1
Porophyllum gracile	X		X	X	3			X		X							X	3	6
Prosopis juliflora v. *torreyana*						X			X									2	2
Prosopis juliflora v. (?)													X			X		2	2
Psilostrophe cooperi												X						1	1

*Column numbers 1 through 16 correspond to table numbers C-1 through C-16.

(cont'd)

TABLE C-17 (cont'd)

Taxa occurrence by transect cluster *

Taxa	*Sonora*				*Cluster Frequency*	*Baja California*												*Cluster Frequency*	*Total Cluster Frequency*
	1	2	3	4		5	6	7	8	9	10	11	12	13	14	15	16		
Rosa minutifolia											X							1	1
Simmondsia chinensis	X		X	X	3	X	X	X	X	X		X						6	9
Solanum hindsianum	X		X	X	3				X	X							X	3	6
Sphaeralcea sp.	X	X	X	X	4									X			X	2	2
Stephanomeria pauciflora	X		X		2														2
Trixis californica			X	X	2												X	1	3
Unknown																	X	1	1
Viguiera deltoidea									X									1	1
Viguiera microphylla														X				1	1
Viguiera purisimae																	X	1	1
Viscainoa geniculata						X												1	1
Xylonagra arborea v. *wigginsii*																	X	1	1
Yucca valida						X												1	1
Yucca whipplei v. *eremica*																X		1	1
Zinnea pumila								X										1	1

*Column numbers 1 through 16 correspond to table numbers C-1 through C-16.

Literature Cited

ALLISON, E. C.

1964 Geology of areas bordering Gulf of California. Pp. 3–29 *in* Marine Geology of the Gulf of California. Am. Assoc. Petroleum Geologists, Memoir 3. Tulsa, Okla.

ANDERSON, D. L.

1971 The San Andreas Fault. Sci. Amer. 225: 53–68.

ASCHMANN, HOMER

1959 The Central Desert of Baja California: demography and ecology. Ibero-Americana 42, Univ. Calif. Press, Berkeley and Los Angeles.

AXELROD, DANIEL I.

1952 A theory of angiosperm evolution. Evolution 6:29–60.

1958 Evolution of the Madro-tertiary geoflora. Bot. Rev. 24:433–509.

1960 The evolution of flowering plants. Pp. 227–235 *in* Evolution after Darwin. v. 1, The Evolution of Life.

BANÇO DO NORDESTE DO BRASIL, S. A.

1964 O Nordeste e as Lavouras Xerofilas. Fortaleza, Ceara, Brasil.

BARRETT, ELLEN C.

1957 Baja California, 1935–1950. Bennett & Marshall, Los Angeles. 284 pp.; inside cover maps.

BENSON, LYMAN

1962 Plant taxonomy, methods and principles. The Ronald Press Co., N.Y.

1969 The cacti of Arizona. Revised 3rd ed. Univ. Ariz. Press, Tucson.

BRANDEGEE, T. S.

1892 Distribution of the flora of the Cape Region of Baja Calif. Zoe 3: 223–231.

BURRUS, ERNEST J.

1967 Wenceslaus Linck's reports and letters, 1762–1778. Translated into English, edited and annotated by Ernest J. Burrus. S. J. Dawson's Book Shop, Los Angeles.

CANFIELD, ELMER R.

1971 University of Arizona. Personal communication.

CANFIELD, R. H.

1942 Sampling ranges by the line interception method. Plant cover-composition-density-degree of forage use. Res. Rept. 4, U. S. Dept. Agr. For. Serv. Southwestern Forest and Range Exp. Sta. Mimeo.

CANNON, RAY & THE SUNSET EDITORS
1966 The Sea of Cortez. Lane Magazine and Book Co., Menlo Park, Calif.
CARROLL, LEWIS (Charles Lutwidge Dodgson)
1966 The hunting of the snark. Pantheon Books, N.Y.
CLAVIGERO, FRANCESCO SAVERIO, S. J.
1789 Storia della California. Opera Postuma. 2 vols. Venice.
CLAVIJERO, FRANCISCO XAVIER
1937 The history of [Lower] California. Translated from the Italian and edited by Sara E. Lake and A. A. Gray. Stanford Univ. Press, Stanford, Calif.
CONTRERAS ARIAS, ALFONSO
1942 Mapas de las provincias climatologicas de la Republica Mexicana. Mexico: Instituto Geografico.
COOPER, CHAS. F.
1957 The variable plot method for estimating shrub density. Journ. Range Management. 10:111–115.
CURRAN, MARY K.
1885 List of the plants described in California, principally in the Proc. of the Calif. Acad. of Sciences, by Dr. Albert Kellogg, Dr. H. H. Behr, and Mr. H. N. Bolander; with an attempt at their classification. Bull. No. 3., Calif. Acad. Sci. 128–151.
DAYTON, W. A.
1931 Important western browse plants. U.S. Dept. Agr. Misc. Publ. No. 101. Govt. Printing Off., Wash. D. C.
1937 Range plant handbook. Govt. Printing Off., Wash., D. C.
DRESSLER, R. L.
1957 The genus Pedilanthus (Euphorbiaceae). Contributions from the Gray Herbarium of Harvard Univ., Cambridge, Mass.
DUEWER, ELIZABETH A.
1971 University of Arizona. Personal communication.
DURHAM, J. W. & E. C. ALLISON
1960 The geologic history of Baja California and its marine faunas. Systematic Zool. 9:47–91.
ENGELMANN, G.
1883 Morphology of spines. Bot. Gaz. 8:338.
ENGLER, A. & HANS MELCHIOR
1966 Syllabus der pflanzenfamilien. Gebruder Borntrager, Berlin. 666 pp.
FEATHERLY, H. I.
1965 Taxonomic terminology of the higher plants. Hafner Publishing Co., N.Y. and London.
GARCIA, ENRIQUETA
1964 Modificaciones al sistema de classificacion climatica de Koppen (para adaptarlo a las condiciones de la Republica Mexicana). Instituto de Geografia de la Univ. Nacional Autonoma de Mexico, Mexico, D.F.
GARCIA, ENRIQUETA & PEDRO A. MOSINO
1968 Los climas de la Baja California. Univ. Nacional Autonoma de Mexico, Instituto de Geofisica, Mexico, D.F.
GARDNER, ERLE STANLEY
1962 The hidden heart of Baja. William Morrow & Co., N.Y.

GENTRY, HOWARD SCOTT

1949 Land plants collected by the VELERO III, Allan Hancock Pacific Expeditions 1937–1941. Univ. Southern Calif. Press, Los Angeles.

GERHARD, PETER & H. E. GULICK

1967 Lower California guidebook, 4th ed. The Arthur H. Clark Co., Glendale, Calif.

GOLDMAN, E. A.

1916 Plant records of an expedition to Lower California. Contributions from the U. S. National Herbarium, vol. 16, pt. 14, pp. 309–316. Govt. Printing Off., Wash., D. C.

GROSENBAUGH, L. R.

1952 Plotless timber estimates — new, fast, easy. Jour. Forestry 50:32–37.

HALL, ROBERT L.

1972 University of Arizona. Personal communication.

HARLAN, ANNITA D. S.

1970 Some aspects of the ecology of *Tillandsia recurvata* L. in southern Arizona. M. S. Thesis, Univ. Ariz., Tucson.

HASTINGS, J. R.

1964 Climatological data for Baja California. Technical reports on the meteorology and climatology of arid regions. No. 14. Institute of Atmospheric Physics, Univ. Ariz., Tucson.

HASTINGS, J. R. & R. R. HUMPHREY

1969a Climatological data and statistics for Baja California. Technical reports on the meteorology and climatology of arid regions. No. 18. Institute of Atmospheric Physics, Univ. Ariz., Tucson.

1969b Climatological data and statistics for Sonora and northern Sinaloa. Technical reports on the meteorology and climatology of arid regions. No. 19. Institute of Atmospheric Physics, Univ. Ariz., Tucson.

HASTINGS, J. R. & R. M. TURNER

1965 Seasonal precipitation regimes in Baja California, Mexico. Geografiska Annaler 47: 204–223.

HENRICKSON, JAMES

1967 Pollen morphology of the Fouquieriaceae. Aliso 6:137–160.

1969 An introduction to the Fouquieriaceae. Cactus and Succulent Journ. of America 41(3):97–105.

1972a California State College, Los Angeles. Personal communication.

1972b A taxonomic revision of the Fouquieriaceae. Aliso 7:439–537.

HOWELL, J. V. *(Coordinating chairman)*

1966 Glossary of geology, with supplement, 2nd ed. Am. Geol. Institute, Wash., D. C.

HUMPHREY, R. R.

1931 Thorn formation in *Fouquieria splendens* and *Idria columnaris*. Bull. Torrey Bot. Club 58:263–264.

1935 A study of *Idria columnaris* and *Fouquieria splendens*. Am. Journ. Bot. 22: 184–207.

1970 Five dominants of the Central Desert of Baja California. Cactus and Succ. Journ. 42: Pt. I, 209–212; Pt. II, 275–279.

1971 Comments on an epiphyte, a parasite and four independent spermatophytes of the Central Desert of Baja California. Cactus and Succ. Journ. 43:99–104.

HUMPHREY, R. R. & A. B. HUMPHREY
1969 Height and volume characteristics of *Idria columnaris* Kellogg. Journ. Ariz. Acad. Sci. 5(4):207–215.
HUMPHREY, R. R. & FLOYD G. WERNER
1969 Some records of bee visitations to the flowers of *Idria columnaris*. Journ. Ariz. Acad. Sci. 5(4):243–244.
JAEGER, EDMUND C.
1957 The North American deserts. Stanford Univ. Press, Stanford, Calif.
JOHNSTON, I. M.
1924 Expedition of the California Academy of Sciences to the Gulf of California in 1921. (The botany of the vascular plants). Proc. Calif. Acad. Sci. IV (12):951–1218.
KELLOGG, ALBERT
1960 *Idria columnaris*. The Hesperian 4(3):101–102.
KRUTCH, JOSEPH WOOD
1961 The forgotten peninsula; a naturalist in Baja California. William Sloan Associates, N.Y.
LARSON, ROGER L., H. W. MENARD, & S. M. SMITH
1968 Gulf of California: a result of ocean-floor spreading and transform faulting. Sci. 161:781–784.
MALLERY, T. D.
1936a Rainfall records for the Sonoran Desert. Ecol. 17:110–121.
1936b Rainfall records for the Sonoran Desert. II. Summary of readings to December 1935. Ecol. 17:212–215.
MARTINEZ, MAXIMINO
1947 Baja California — Reseña histórica del territorio y de su flora. Ediciones Botas, Mexico.
MEIGS, PEVERIL
1966 Geography of coastal deserts. UNESCO, Paris. Arid Zone Research 28.
MOORE, D. G. & E. C. BUFFINGTON
1968 Transform faulting and growth of the Gulf of California since the Late Pliocene. Sci. 161:1238–1241.
MORAN, REID
1968 Cardon. Pac. Discovery 21(2) 2–9.
NASH, G. V.
1903 A revision of the family Fouquieriaceae. Bull. Torr. Bot. Club 30: 449–459.
NELSON, E. W.
1922 Lower California and its natural resources. Natl. Acad. Sci. Vol. 16.
ORCUTT, C. R.
1886 *Fouquieria gigantea,* new species. W. Am. Scientist 2:48.
POISSON, M. J.
1895 Note sur le developpment des épines de l'*Idria columnaris*. Bull. Mus. Nat. Hist. I:278–279.
REICHE, K.
1922 Beitrage zur Kenntnis der Gattung *Fouquieria*. Botanische Jahrbuchen 57: 287–301.

ROBINSON, W. J.
1904 The spines of *Fouquieria*. Bull. Torrey Bot. Club 31:45–50.

RUSNAK, GENE A. & ROBERT L. FISHER
1964 Structural history and evolution of Gulf of California. Pp. 144–156 *in* Marine Geology of the Gulf of California. Am. Assoc. Petroleum Geologists Memoir 3. Tulsa, Okla.

SAUER, CARL O. & PEVERIL MEIGS
1927 Lower California studies: I. Site and culture at San Fernando Velicata. Univ. Calif. Publ. Geogr. 2:271–302.

SHREVE, FORREST
1931 Die Fouquieraceen. Die Pflanzenareale 1: 3–4.
1937 The vegetation of the Cape Region of Baja California. Madroña IV (4): 105–113.
1951 Vegetation of the Sonoran Desert. Carnegie Inst. of Wash. Publ. 591. Wash., D. C.

SHREVE, FORREST & I. L. WIGGINS
1964 Vegetation and flora of the Sonoran Desert. 2 vols. Stanford Univ. Press, Stanford, Calif.

STANDLEY, PAUL C.
1920–26 Trees and shrubs of Mexico. Govt. Printing Off., Wash., D. C.

STEARN, WILLIAM T.
1966 Botanical Latin. Hafner Publ. Co., N.Y.

STRONG, CHARLES W.
1966 An improved method of obtaining density from line-transect data. Ecol. 47(2):311–313.

THOMSON, JOHN W.
1971 University of Wisconsin. Personal communication.

U. S. DEPARTMENT OF AGRICULTURE
1941 Climate and man: Yearbook Agric., 1941. Govt. Printing Off., Wash., D. C.

VAN TIEGHEM, P.
1899 Sur les Fouquieriacees. Jour. Bot. 13:293–301.

VIVO, JORGE A. & JOSE C. GOMEZ
1946 Climatologia de Mexico. Mexico: Instituto Panamericano de Geografia e Historia.

Index